AQA

GCSE ENGLISH

Students' Book

Rachel Redford

AQA ENGLISH/ENGLISH MATURE

SPECIFICATION B

OXFORD
UNIVERSITY PRESS

Great Clarendon Street, Oxford OX2 6DP

Oxford University Press is a department of the University of Oxford. It furthers the University's objective of excellence in research, scholarship, and education by publishing worldwide in

Oxford New York

Auckland Bangkok Buenos Aires Cape Town Chennai Dar es Salaam Delhi Hong Kong Istanbul Karachi Kolkata Kuala Lumpur Madrid Melbourne Mexico City Mumbai Nairobi São Paulo Shanghai Taipei Tokyo Toronto

Oxford is a registered trade mark of Oxford University Press in the UK and in certain other countries

British Library Cataloguing in Publication Data

Data available

ISBN 0 19 831897 9

10 9 8 7 6 5 4 3 2

Printed in Italy by Rotolito Lombarda

Acknowledgments

The Publisher would like to thank the following for permission to reproduce photographs:

Academy of Natural Sciences of Philadelphia/Corbis UK Ltd: p 37; Alamy.com: p 50; Tony Annis: p 29; Associated Press/Darko Bandic: p 19; Associated Press/Tanya Makeyeva: p 11; Associated Press/Enric Marti: p 12; Corel Professional Photos: pp 54 (top), 55 (top), 58 (top), 62, 69, 64, 81, 83, 96 (middle & bottom); Digital Vision: pp 54 (bottom), 55 (bottom), 58 (bottom); FPG International/Getty Images Creative: p 74; The Image Bank/Getty Images Creative: p 80; Photodisc: pp 78, 86, 94; Popperfoto: p 9; WSPA: p 13; Stockbyte: p 96 (top).

Front/back Cover: Alamy.com (background), Popperfoto (bottom), Corel Professional Photos (bottom middle), Corbis UK Ltd (top middle) & Hulton Archive (Top)

Artwork: Benoit Jacques mobile phone illustration, copyright © Benoit Jacques 2001, published in The Guardian 'Weekend', 8.12.01, copyright © Benoit Jacques 2001, reprinted by permission of the artist. p 20. 'Whoof whoof' by 'Snaffles', from Plain Tales from the Raj. Ed. Charles Allen 1975: p 34.

We are grateful for permission to include the following copyright material in this book:

Charles Allen: extract from Plain Tales from the Raj: Images of British India in the Twentieth Century (Andre Deutsch/BBC, 1995), reprinted by permission of the Carlton Publishing Group.

Adriaan Barnouw translation from the Dutch of Petrus Augustus de Genestet: 'Such is Holland!' from Coming After: An Anthology of Poetry from the Low Countries (1948), copyright © 1948 by The Trustees of Rutgers College in New Jersey, reprinted by permission of the publishers, Rutgers University Press.

Martin Bell: extract from In Harm's Way (Hamish Hamilton, 1995), copyright © Martin Bell 1995, reprinted by permission of Penguin Books Ltd.

Jean 'Binta' Breeze: 'just in case' from The Arrival of Brighteye and Other Poems (Bloodaxe Books, 2000), reprinted by permission of the publishers.

Dr Ian Gibson MP: 'We were told there was no risk to humans' published in the Sunday Mirror, 26.3.00, reprinted by permission of the author.

George Monbiot: 'An unfair exchange', copyright © George Monbiot 1999, published in The Guardian, 15.5.99, reprinted by permission of the author.

Blake Morrison: 'Silence is Golden', copyright © Blake Morrison 2001, published in The Guardian 'Weekend', 8.12.01, reprinted by permission of Guardian Newspapers Ltd.

Les Murray: 'One in a Lifetime, Snow' from Collected Poems (1991), reprinted by permission of Carcanet Press Ltd.

Lorna Sage: extract from Bad Blood (4th Estate, 2000), copyright © Lorna Sage 2000, reprinted by permission of HarperCollins Publishers Ltd.

Vikram Seth: 'The Eagle and the Beetle' from Beastly Tales from Here and There (Phoenix, 1993), reprinted by permission of The Orion Publishing Group Ltd.

Abdulah Sidran: 'A Blind Man Sings to His City' from Scar on the Stone: Contemporary Poetry from Bosnia, translated by Ted Hughes and Antonela Glavinic (Bloodaxe, 2000), reprinted by permission of Abdulah Sidran, Antonela Glavinic and Faber & Faber Ltd on behalf of the Estate of Ted Hughes.

Marin Sorescu: 'Mal du Pays' from Censored Poems translated by John Hartley Williams & Hilde Offschofski (Bloodaxe Books, 2001), reprinted by permission of the publishers.

Lisa Sykes: extract from 'The Essential Guide to: Cycling holidays', published in Wanderlust June/July 2001, reprinted by permission of the author.

and also to the following for their permission:

Atlantic Syndication for 'Kabul's bear with no nose' by Barbara Jones from Mail on Sunday, 25.11.01; and 'Pride of Kabul who took on the Taliban and won' by Chris Stephen from Evening Standard, 20.11.01.

Mirror Group for headlines from the Sunday Mirror 26.3.00.

New Internationalist, www.newint.org, for 'Side by side in destitution' by Olivia Ward from New Internationalist 341, December 2001.

WSPA UK for article 'WSPA disaster relief team on standby' from WSPA UK website 06.12.01

It has not been possible to trace and contact all copyright holders of material included before publication. If notified the publisher undertakes to rectify any errors or omissions at the earliest opportunity.

CONTENTS

PREFACE FOR TEACHERS

From 2004, the English examination papers will change in accordance with the new specifications. This book will guide students – and teachers – through the kinds of tasks they will meet.

In the Reading Section of this Students' Book, for both tiers, there are examples of media and non-fiction texts, and poetry from different cultures. They have been chosen to demonstrate the sort of texts which students will meet in the pre-released booklet and the examination papers – and to provide real interest and challenge to both students and teachers.

Students are given clear guidance on writing responses to the kinds of questions they are likely to meet on the examination papers, and this guidance is carefully structured to build the skills of both foundation and higher tier students.

The Writing Section presents, in six separate units, the two triplets 'argue, persuade, advise' and 'analyse, review, comment' which are targeted in the examination. In each unit, advice and guidance are given on structuring an answer to an examination type task. A student's exemplar response is provided followed by an examiner's detailed commentary written in accessible language. Students can use this commentary as a checklist when they write their own responses to the examination type task provided for them at the end of each unit.

I hope that this book will enable your students to perform to their full potential, and achieve success in their English GCSE examination. I hope, too, that you and your students *enjoy* using it. I believe that you will.

Rachel Redford

Rachel Redford

MEDIA INTRODUCTION

You will first meet your media texts in your **pre-released booklet**. The booklet will contain a range of texts on a topic which has recently been in the news. It could, for example, be coverage of the war in Afghanistan. The texts will be reproduced in their original layout. The texts will be different every year, but could include:

- news stories from national and local newspapers
- images and cartoons
- newspaper editorials and letters
- web pages

You will have your pre-released booklet for four months before the examination. In class you will, therefore, be able to discuss and write about the media texts, so you will have a close knowledge and understanding of them before you sit the examination.

Starting with the examination in 2005, you will not be allowed to write any notes or comments on your pre-released booklet.

Your **media texts** will be examined on Paper 1 in Section A. The question will have several parts to it and you won't know which texts you will be asked to write about until you read it. The question will direct you to particular texts.

So, you're in the examination hall with your examination question in front of you. What should you do?

REMINDING YOURSELF OF THE TEXTS

You can't afford to waste any time, so read the whole question immediately and then focus on each part of the question in turn. You will need to refer to texts and layout in the pre-released booklet. You should be thoroughly familiar with them, so you will need only to refresh your memory. You should have a general idea of your answer as soon as you have read the question, so you can then go through the target texts at speed to find appropriate brief quotations and supporting detail.

WRITING YOUR ANSWER

Some important 'DOs':
- DO make sure that every sentence you write answers **relevantly** the question you are being asked
- DO use the correct technical terms, as it saves words
- DO be **concise** and **economical**
- DO be **analytical** – Explain! Explore! Comment! Analyse!
- DO use detail, and give examples from the texts and layout to make your points
- DO use **brief** quotations clearly linked to the points you are making

And some important 'DON'Ts':
- DON'T write out the question – you will only waste time
- DON'T waste words on **narrating** the content or **describing** the presentation of the texts
- DON'T quote at length – quote words and phrases, not whole lines

CHECKLIST

The following is a useful checklist. You will meet these topics and terms as you work through the media assignments in this book. When you have finished the assignments, it would be helpful to go through this list to make sure you understand them and can use them in your writing.

Media layout or presentation
- Photographs/images/pictures – analyse their position on the page, and their appeal
- Image captions – are they emotive, factual, humorous?
- Headlines – do they use puns? Are they shocking or dramatic?
- Sub-headings and bylines – look at style and content
- Font size – is this used for effect?
- What use is made of bold or italic type?
- Are illustrations (e.g. graphs, maps, logos) informative or persuasive?
- Cartoons – what visual cues do they use? How important are their captions?

Content and purpose
- Opinions and arguments – are they biased, impartial, personal, controversial? Are they intended to: persuade, inform, shock, change the reader's opinion?
- Narrative news reporting – is it dramatic, emotional, full of

suspense? Is it intended to: entertain, inform, involve the reader emotionally?

◆ Analysis of issues — are these issues political, social, personal, global? Are texts intended to: inform, analyse, question, explore?

Language used for effect

◆ Imagery — how is it used (e.g. metaphors, similes, alliteration)?

◆ Modifiers (adjectives, adverbs) — are they single, multiple, hyphenated?

◆ Technical or specialist vocabulary — how is it used?

◆ Verbs — are they active, passive, imperative?

◆ Word length — are words short/long; monosyllabic/polysyllabic?

◆ Vocabulary — is it emotive, impartial, factual?

Organization

◆ Sentences — are they short/long for effect? Do they use subordinate clauses?

◆ Punctuation — are there parenthetical commas, semi-colons, exclamation marks, continuation dots, question marks, quotation marks, dashes?

◆ Paragraphs — are they short/long? What is the position of the topic sentence? Are there connecting words between them?

◆ Connectives — are these words and phrases used to mark textual stages?

◆ Are introductory and concluding sentences/paragraphs used effectively?

MEDIA UNIT 1

ASSIGNMENT

◆ Explain the difficulties experienced by the animals, and by those looking after them, which are described by Chris Stephen and Barbara Jones.

◆ How effective is the layout of the two newspaper articles?

◆ Compare the purpose of Barbara Jones in writing 'Kabul's bear with no nose' with the purpose of the writer of the WSPA website page.

The texts for this assignment are on pages 11–13.

Look at the first part of the assignment:

◆ Explain the difficulties experienced by the animals, and by those looking after them, which are described by Chris Stephen and Barbara Jones.

Read through the two articles. Now re-read them and, as you read, write down a list of the difficulties which the animals and their keepers have had to suffer. You could start your list as you read 'Pride of Kabul' in this way:

a) The lion had stones, rockets and a grenade thrown at him

b) The elephant house and the aquarium were destroyed in a rocket attack

When you have finished your list, organize the material you have written. Plan one paragraph on attacks on the animals, and another on problems with feeding. In this way, you won't repeat yourself and your answer will be structured.

Now you've completed the first part of the assignment and are ready for the next part:

◆ How effective is the layout of the two newspaper articles?

KEY TERM

Layout is the effective use of pictures, headlines, and headings. The function of these media features is to catch the attention of the reader.

First of all, look at the pictures of the wounded lion and bear. You can't help looking at them closely: at the lion's smashed face and the bear's sliced off nose. Why are the images so arresting? What do they make you feel? Whether they make you say 'Ugh!' or 'Aaah!', they have an **emotional impact** on you.

Write down the answers to the following questions:
1. How does the gaze of both animals involve the reader?
2. What does the positioning of the bear's paws say to you?
3. What qualities of his character does the picture of the lion keeper convey?

Next, look at the headlines and headings.

Write down the answers to the following:
1. How does the choice of words in the heading 'Kabul's bear with no nose' stir the feelings of horror, pity and anger in the reader?
2. How does the choice of words in the heading 'Pride of Kabul who took on the Taliban and won' suggest the lion's courage?
3. Headlines often use puns. Find a pun in the headline 'Pride of Kabul' and explain why it is effective.

KEY TERM

A **pun** is a play on words, where somebody uses words that are exactly the same, or sound the same, but have different meanings. This is often for humorous effect, e.g. 'I'm on a seafood diet: I see food and I eat it'.

4. Pick out two **emotive** words from the caption under the picture of the bear, and explain why they are both emotive and effective.

You can now use all the points you have made in answer to these questions, and the questions themselves, to write your response to this part of the assignment.

Finally, look at the third part of the assignment:

◆ Compare the purpose of Barbara Jones in writing 'Kabul's bear with no nose' with the purpose of the writer of the WSPA website page.

Why do you think Barbara Jones wrote 'Kabul's bear with no nose'? Write down your ideas by completing the following:

1. What did the writer want to **inform** us about?
2. Explain the range of **emotions** that the writer wanted us to feel.
3. Summarize the writer's **main** purpose in writing the article.

When it comes to the WSPA website page, the link headings at the top tell us clearly why it was written:

DONATIONS /GET INVOLVED / ABOUT US / WHAT WE DO /
NEWS / CONTACT US / STAY INFORMED / SEARCH

What is the **tone** of these capitalized link headings?

KEY TERM

Tone is the word used to describe the mood, feel or atmosphere of a
piece of writing, e.g. sad or funny.

These link headlines are not asking you to feel sorry for the animals,
or to feel outrage at how cruelly they have suffered. The **tone** is
different. It is businesslike and organized.

Write down your answers to the following:
1. Having read these website page link headings, what would you
   expect to get from the website?
2. Pick out the link headings which are **imperative verbs**. What
   relationship do they establish between the reader and the website?

KEY TERM

Imperative verbs are verbs in their command form, e.g. 'Help the
unfortunate animals'.

3. Comment on the effectiveness of the brevity of the link headings.
4. Explain how the link headings summarize the purpose of the
   website.

Now read the rest of the website page and summarize concisely how
the website writer involves the reader.

Now you can compare this evidence with your analysis of Barbara
Jones's purpose in writing 'Kabul's bear with no nose'. Using
quotations and your answers to these questions, explain:
1. the purpose of Barbara Jones's article
2. the purpose of the website page
3. in what ways the purposes are similar and different.

You have now completed the assignment.

Evening Standard 20 November 2001

BATTLE FOR AFGHANISTAN

Pride of Kabul who took on the Taliban and won

From Chris Stephen in Kabul

1. Marjan the lion, star of Kabul Zoo, has survived rocket attacks by the Mujahideen, stoning by the Taliban, and a grenade thrown by the brother of a man whose arm he ate. Now the zoo hopes the ousting of the Taliban means an expert will fly in and treat the lion's ailments.

2. Marjan arrived in Kabul as a present from the former West Germany when Afghanistan was at peace, under the rule of King Zahir Shah. But the Soviet invasion brought war from 1979-1989 and the zoo decayed. Things got worse in 1992 when the Mujahideen ousted the Moscow-backed regime, took Kabul, and began fighting among themselves.

3. Warlord Gulbuddin Hekmatyar, who was kept out of the city, took his revenge with a rocket bombardment. One rocket hit the elephant house. Another took out the aquarium near the pen Marjan shared with a lioness, Quanni.

4. Head zookeeper, Sher Agha, said: 'There were so many rockets we evacuated everyone. There was just a security guard. For the animals, we would get the food together and in a lull drive in and feed them as fast as possible.'

5. During this time of chaos an intruder jumped into the lions' cage. Marjan bit off his arm and the man died. A few days later the man's brother lobbed a grenade into Marjan's pen. Splinters tore into Marjan's legs, slashed his mouth and blinded him in one eye.

6. In 1996, the Mujahideen were kicked out of Kabul by the Taliban. Visiting Taliban threw stones at Marjan and as food shortages began to bite in Afghanistan, the deer and rabbits were taken and eaten. For Marjan, loneliness arrived with the death two years ago of Quanni the lioness.

7. Mr Agha has to borrow money to buy the animals food. But he is hopeful. 'I have 19 creatures and I love them all but Marjan is the one I love best,' he said 'I just hope somebody will now come and take a look at Marjan.'

The Mail on Sunday 25 November 2001

After the one-eyed Lion of Kabul, another Taliban outrage in the Afghan zoo...

Kabul's bear with no nose

TORTURED: Khers, who was attacked by Taliban thugs

❶ With the remains of her nose raw and bloodied, Khers the bear claws the bars of her cage, plainly in agony.

❷ Pictured here for the first time, the four-year-old Afghan black bear is one of only 17 animals left at battered Kabul Zoo.

❸ She was tortured with sticks and, in an act of unimaginable cruelty, her nose tip was cut off with a bayonet by bored Taliban soldiers while they still controlled the Afghan capital.

❹ Her horrified keeper, Sher Agha, was unable to stop them taking swipes at the helpless creature and causing an open, fleshy wound. The injury is so deep, there is still a danger of it becoming badly infected.

❺ 'She is a poor little animal,' said Sher. 'She hasn't hurt anyone and yet, when the Taliban were here they used to come in just to torment the animals.

❻ 'Whenever my back was turned, they would take a stick and hit her hard.'

❼ Once the zoo boasted a fine aquarium and had 40 species on show. But years of conflict and neglect have left the buildings in ruins. Bars on at least half the animal cages are twisted beyond

From
Barbara Jones
in Kabul

repair and doors hang open from broken hinges.

❽ And yet, thanks to the determination and bravery of 11 dedicated staff – who have run out of money, and haven't been paid since July – the battered little zoo has just about managed to survive.

❾ The Mail on Sunday has now teamed up with the international animal charity WSPA (World Society for the Protection of Animals) to get urgently needed food and emergency medical treatment to the animals.

❿ The Born Free Foundation has also pledged to send aid.

⓫ The plight of the zoo was brought to the world's attention last week largely because of Marjan, the 15-stone one-eyed lion, another pitiful victim of violence in Afghanistan.

⓬ He lost his eye and was badly wounded in the early Nineties when an Afghan threw a grenade in his pit in revenge for the lion

eating his brother, who was teasing him.

⓭ Mr Agha said: 'It has been a terrible struggle just keeping him, the bear and all the others alive when there has been a shortage of food for all of us here in Kabul city.

⓮ 'Recently, there was constant bombing, unnerving all the animals here.

⓯ 'But it is the bear and Marjan I feel most sorry for. I've been spending extra time with them during the recent air strikes and all the shelling and gunfire in the streets.'

⓰ The Mail on Sunday yesterday also arranged for one of the best vets in the country, Abdul Rahman, to examine Marjan and treat Khers the bear's nose to prevent it becoming infected.
He will be making regular visits to the animals.

Additional reporting: Elizabeth Sanderson

Back | Forward | Stop | Refresh | Home | AutoFill | Print | Mail | Favorites

Address: http://www.wspa.org.uk/afghanistan/

WSPA
World Society for the Protection of Animals

DONATIONS • GET INVOLVED • ABOUT US • WHAT WE DO • NEWS • CONTACT US • STAY INFORMED • SEARCH

WSPA disaster relief team on standby

1 In response to increasing reports of the plight of Afghanistan's animals, including those at Kabul zoo, WSPA is preparing to mobilize an animal disaster relief team to visit the country at the earliest possible opportunity.

2 In the short term, WSPA has committed several thousand dollars from its disaster relief fund and is trying to find a way of getting this money into Afghanistan to enable the animals at Kabul zoo to be fed and cared for until this transitional period is over and funding from the municipality is resumed.

3 In Afghanistan as a whole, WSPA suspects that large numbers of livestock and other animals may have been killed or injured as a result of the conflict. It is also likely that rabies may become more of a problem, due to the increasing numbers of stray dogs in the region.

4 John Walsh, WSPA's international projects director, said, 'The current crisis in Afghanistan has become a terrible tragedy for the people of the region and their animals.

5 'In situations like this, WSPA has a long track record in working to address the problems facing the livestock and pet animal populations. During the previous conflict in Afghanistan, a WSPA team visited the Kabul zoo and provided medical treatment for the animals there. WSPA is committed to doing all it can to alleviate their suffering now.'

Kabul Update
December 2001

6 WSPA has now managed to get funds to Kabul zoo through the Mail on Sunday newspaper. WSPA has pledged an initial sum of around £2,000 which was sent to the Zoo Director, Sher Agha, through a Mail on Sunday reporter.

7 In consultation with the Director of the British Zoo Federation, WSPA estimates that the cost of running the zoo would be around $1,000 a month. WSPA will commit to paying for the animals' food for the next 6 months.

Join WSPA by Direct Debit for only £3 a month!
Call our helpline or post your direct debit mandate to us.

Make a donation
Make a donation online or by post.

Get involved
How you can help make a difference. Take action and raise money on our behalf.

DONATIONS • GET INVOLVED • ABOUT US • WHAT WE DO • NEWS • CONTACT US • STAY INFORMED • SEARCH

Internet zone

Favorites | History | Search | Scrapbook | Page Holder

MEDIA UNIT 2

ASSIGNMENT

Write about the two media texts under the following headings:
◆ the writer's purpose and language in 'We were told there was no risk to humans'
◆ the effectiveness of the layout of the 'We were told there was no risk to humans' page
◆ the writer's opinions in 'Silence is golden'
◆ how the cartoonist makes his point

The texts for this assignment are on pages 19–20.

First of all, think about:

◆ The writer's purpose and language in 'We were told there was no risk to humans'

EXAMINER'S TIP A writer's purpose and language are linked together. The kind of language a writer uses depends on **why** he or she is writing.

You must decide why Dr Gibson wrote this article.
Your answer should include the following points:

a) to inform the reader about the research being carried out on the adverse effects of mobile phones
b) to give the reader facts about NRPB findings which conflict with the current research on mobile phones
c) to convince the reader that the NRPB's conclusions that mobile phones do not have adverse effects on health should be questioned
d) to make the reader aware of the possible dangers of mobile phones

Dr Gibson's purpose is obviously a serious one. You can, therefore, expect the writer to use **factual** language.

Work through the following questions, leaving three lines blank after your answer for each one.

Vocabulary

Nouns:
1. Are they concrete or abstract?
2. Are they specialized or technical?
3. Are they easily understood?

4.   Are they modified?

Verbs:
5.   Are they active or passive?
6.   Do they suggest or do they state?

Sentence structure

7.   Are the sentences of varying length?
8.   Do they contain subordinate clauses?

Subordinate clauses add more information to the main clause, e.g. 'I'll phone you <u>when I have some news</u>.'

Paragraphing

9.   Are the paragraphs short or long?
10. Are they indented?
11. Are connectives used?

Connectives are linking words, e.g. furthermore, therefore, however, finally.

Now fill in the blanks in your answers with your explanation of the **effect** of these features. For example, following your answer on concrete and abstract nouns, you could write:

The many abstract nouns have the effect of making the text thoughtful. They appeal to the reader's sense of judgement. This is appropriate because the text is about facts and opinions.

When you have filled in all your blanks, you have completed this part of the assignment. You're now ready for the second part:

◆ The effectiveness of the layout of the 'We were told there was no risk to humans' page

Layout is intended to catch the reader's eye so that the newspaper will be bought and read. You will need to comment on the effect of layout features, such as:
a)   the picture of the soldier with a mobile
b)   the spread of the previous *Sunday Mirror* headlines
c)   the headline and caption
d)   the words used to describe the writer

EXAMINER'S
TIP Before you start, use a dictionary to help you to write down the definitions of the following adjectives, so that you can use them when you explain the effectiveness of the layout: dramatic, emotive, alarmist, emphatic, and arresting.

You can now start writing about the layout. As an example, the first one has been started for you:

a)   the picture of the soldier with a mobile

a) The picture of the soldier with his mobile dominates the page.
    It is an arresting image, which grabs the reader's attention. ...

Work through the features listed in this way and you have completed the second part of the assignment.

Now look at the third part of the assignment:

◆ The writer's opinions in 'Silence is golden'

KEY
TERM   An **opinion** is a belief, a view or a judgement about something or someone. For example, one person might feel that mobile phones are a wonderful convenience; someone else might think that mobiles are a nuisance because they disturb the peace of train travellers; someone else might firmly believe they cause cancer. Everyone is entitled to his or her own opinion.

Before you can explain the writer's opinions in 'Silence is golden', you have to read the article carefully. As you read for the first time, write down the words you do not know, or are not sure of. When you have finished reading, you will probably have quite a long list, because this is the most difficult text in this unit. You might have begun your list with:

a) Disparaging
b) Eroded
c) Taciturn

When you have completed your list of unfamiliar words, use a dictionary to write down the definitions of these words which best fit the way they are used in this text. You will need to refer back to the text as you look up the words. When you feel that you understand the listed words, read the text again.

Now you can think about the writer's opinions. To extract the writer's opinions here, you need to summarize the appropriate parts of the text. Writing down the answers to the questions below will help you.

Paragraph 1

1. List all the words in the paragraph used to describe a 'quiet' person.
2. What change does the writer think has taken place in the way people regard a quiet person?

Paragraph 2

3. What does the writer think is the difference between being '*less emotionally repressed*' and '*more talkative*'?
4. What fear does the writer feel for people who '*prefer to hold their tongue*'?

Paragraph 3

5. Why is the writer '*opposed to silence*'?
6. What does he believe is the value of television shows like *Big Brother*?

Paragraph 4

7. Why does the writer feel that those who like their own company and don't want to join in phone-ins are at risk?

Paragraph 5

8. What did the writer dread when he was at school?

Paragraph 6

9. How does the writer think people in the train react when they hear his mobile conversation?

Paragraph 7

10. How does the writer feel about other train travellers' mobile conversations?

Paragraph 8

11. What does the writer think may have turned us '*into a nation of blabbers*'?
12. What does the choice of the word '*blabber*' tell the reader about how the writer regards all this talking?

From your answers to the questions above, **select** the parts that tell you about the writer's opinions. Write your answer, explaining his opinions in clear sentences. Quote words and phrases to support your points.

Now look at the final part of the assignment:

◆ How the cartoonist makes his point

First of all, you need to understand what the cartoonist's point is. You can see what the picture is - a train compartment of people are all talking happily on their mobile phones, except for one glum-looking person. The cartoonist is not merely illustrating the article. He intends the picture to convey a message about people's social behaviour. What is this message or point?

Summarize the point in one clear, brief sentence beginning:

The cartoonist's point is to show that . . .

For example, you could complete the sentence this way:

. . . people on trains these days just chat into their mobiles and ignore each other.

The cartoonist doesn't use words and sentences, so what does he use to make his point? Following your summary of the cartoonist's point, now explain in two concise sentences **how** he puts that point across.

These words and phrases will help you: visual representation, visual cues, facial expression, interpretation, isolated, society.

You have now completed the assignment.

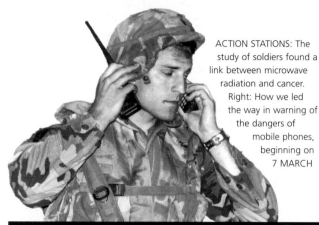

ACTION STATIONS: The study of soldiers found a link between microwave radiation and cancer. Right: How we led the way in warning of the dangers of mobile phones, beginning on 7 MARCH

Sunday Mirror 26 March 2000

MOBILE PHONES COULD MAKE YOUR BRAKES FAIL

SWITCH OFF YOUR MOBILES UNION WARNS STAFF

NEW PROOF MOBILES MAKE YOU LOSE YOUR MEMORY

'We were told there was no risk to humans … this may not be true'

Mobile phones transmit and receive microwave radiation. However, the National Radiological Protection Board (NRPB) concluded in 1990 that, provided exposure was within guideline levels, there should be no adverse effects on health.

The House of Commons Science and Technology Select Committee called for rigorous assessment of the existing research to identify areas in need of further investigation, so that the public can receive clear advice on any risks.

And the NRPB reported there was no human evidence of a risk of cancer resulting from exposure to radiation arising from the use of mobile phones.

The report by Polish scientists has shown that this may not be true. Although the research does not include mobile phones, it shows that the same type of radiation as produced by mobile phones can cause a range of cancers including of the skin and brain.

This work by scientists is preliminary but should result in alarm bells ringing in the heads of the 24 million people in the UK with mobile phones.

By Dr Ian Gibson MP

Member of the Select Committee on Science and Technology

It has been claimed that children may be more susceptible to the effects of microwave radiation.

The research currently under way will take two to three years to complete but we must ensure it is free from industrial influence,

The experience has always been that, whether it is chemicals or radiation, 'safe' levels are always lowered after research is carried out.

Whilst this link is with cancer there is also preliminary evidence that there may be effects on brain function (headaches and memory loss, dizziness, etc.). It's going to be hard to persuade people to give up their phones but it looks like it will become a question of health before convenience.

It was agreed by the Select Committee that the Government must put much more money into research involving the use of mobile phones by children.

We also need to look at the effects of microwave radiation on young people living near mobile masts.

It is suspected that these masts may be associated with childhood leukaemia but much more research needs to be carried out.

There are also, under the Fifth Framework Initiative of the European Commission, large pots of money available for research into microwave radiation. British scientists must be encouraged to bid for this by the Government.

It is certainly true that unless this research is carried out on a wide scale we will never find out the health problems.

The third generation of mobile phones and research into them is now under way and it will be increasingly necessary to ensure that these new phones produce less microwave radiation.

There have been success stories and they will certainly grow in numbers as groups of concerned parents and tenants protest about the siting of masts on tower blocks, schools and streets.

At least 150 MPs have signed a motion expressing deep concern about these issues and many government departments are engaged in reports as a way of allaying fears among the public.

The media has taken up the issue and this is to be welcomed, giving up-to-date facts in an area which is of equal concern as genetically modified food.

The Guardian Weekend 8 December 2001

SILENCE IS GOLDEN

Blake Morrison

1. 'Oh, he's very reserved,' a friend said of a friend the other day. The adjective was meant to be pitying and disparaging, but it was odd to hear it used at all. In the new millennium, 'reserved' is a sign stuck on the better restaurant tables, not a quality found in people. It's not that reserve – quietness, self-containment, the silent assertion of the right to privacy – has ceased to exist. There are still shy people about. But their frail sense of self-worth has been eroded. If someone's taciturn, the suspicion is that he or she has something to hide. The quiet brigade, withdrawn to start with, are in retreat.

2. It's a cliché that Britain, since the death of Princess Diana, has become less emotionally repressed. In truth, we're just more talkative. When I was growing up, saying nowt was a way to stay out of trouble. And, for some kids – those with stammers – speaking was a physical ordeal. Thanks to the growth of speech therapy, stammering is in decline. We're all expected to talk freely and fluently. But what of those who prefer to hold their tongue? Will they become the lepers of tomorrow?

3. Politically, I'm opposed to silence, associating it with cold war paranoia, repressive government and skeletons in the closet. And, aesthetically, I prefer big mouths to tight lips. True, the new garrulity isn't always edifying. But the Jerry Springer Show and Big Brother are a price worth paying if ordinary people get to tell their stories, many

of which aren't ordinary at all. Speech is a kind of therapy in itself. Better out than in.

4. The downside of this is the denigration of those who won't join in the candid fun. Why should they? Not everyone wants to be a caller to the Talk UK Phone-In Show. Nor is a man who prefers his own company necessarily dangerous or mad. Whenever there's a murder case these days, the media like to emphasise how 'quiet' the accused was, how much of a 'loner', as though the habit of solitude were the mark of a killer – not, as it used to be, of a poet.

5. As a teenager, my great dread was being made to speak in front of the other boys at grammar school. Sometimes, even silence was no help: a teacher spotted me blushing after he'd said the word 'sex' and drew the class's mocking attention to it. I was still blushing at the word when it was said in mixed company, years later. Shrinking violet stuff. It was why I started writing poems – because I couldn't make conversation.

6. These days, I can stand in front of large numbers of people and not get butterflies. But the old shyness hasn't quite gone. To engage in a phone conversation, for instance, I need a sound-proofed room or glassed-in telephone kiosk. But like 90% of the nation, I now own a mobile, and the mobile takes malicious pleasure in going off on the train, with commuters around to listen to my half of the dialogue. What narcissism, I tell myself: these people are strangers, they don't give a damn, and anyway, it's only the garage calling about the exhaust pipe.

7. And it's true. No one seems to be listening. For one thing, they're too busy with their own calls. But haven't I listened to their conversations? The girl telling her mate about doing it with her boyfriend last night. The man on the train to Norwich telling his wife he was stuck in Birmingham and wouldn't be back that night. Amazing stuff, spoken at full volume and without a trace of inhibition, and making me resolve never to use my mobile again.

8. Maybe it's mobiles that have turned us into a nation of blabbers. Certainly, trains are much more fun these days: the passengers mightn't talk to each other but they'll say anything to their Nokias. I must tell my friend to buy her friend one for Christmas. Either that, or get him on email. The new technology is bound to cure him of his reserve.

MEDIA UNIT 3

ASSIGNMENT

◆ *Long-distance travel involves a cultural exchange*. Explain how Monbiot argues against this statement in 'An unfair exchange'.

◆ Compare the intentions of the writers of 'An unfair exchange' and 'Side by side in destitution'.

◆ How effective is the photograph accompanying the introduction to 'The essential guide to cycling holidays'?

◆ Analyse the writer's aim and language in the introduction to the cycling holidays article.

The texts for this assignment are on pages 27–29.

Look at the first part of the assignment:

◆ *Long-distance travel involves a cultural exchange*. Explain how Monbiot argues against this statement in 'An unfair exchange'.

The title of this article tells you immediately that the writer disagrees with the above statement. The title states clearly that the exchange between tourists and the host country is '*unfair*'. This means that one party gets a great deal more than the other. In this case, it is obviously we, the tourists, who come off best and the local people who are exploited.

So, what points does Monbiot make to construct his argument? First of all, read the article through. Then, using a dictionary to help you, write down the definitions of the following words and phrases, as they are used in the article: '*ethical*' (para. 1), '*precipitates*' (para. 2), '*compounded*' (para. 3), '*adept*' (para. 4), '*dispossessed*' (para. 4), '*in deficit*' (para. 5), '*unethical*' (para. 7), '*low-impact tourism*' (para. 8), '*counteracting*' (para. 8), '*eco-friendliness*' (para. 8).

Now, read the article again. This time you are going to trace how the writer makes his case against the statement. Stop at the end of each paragraph and **select** any relevant points from it.

Using your own words and including brief quotations, summarize the writer's argument in each paragraph. You could start like this:

Paragraph 1. We don't go abroad for ethical reasons – we go 'to enjoy ourselves'. There is no idea of cultural exchange here.

Paragraph 2. We get to see some aspects of the host country's culture. In exchange they get a few coins and see how rude we can be, but they don't see _our_ culture. This isn't a fair exchange.

Complete these summaries for all nine paragraphs. Then, using these summaries and quotations, complete your answer in clear sentences.

Look at the second part of the assignment:

◆ Compare the intentions of the writers of 'An unfair exchange' and 'Side by side in destitution'.

EXAMINER'S TIP

You are often asked to explain the **intentions** of a writer. This means that you have to decide **why** or for **what purpose** a particular text was written. What did the writer want to achieve? Before you answer that, it is helpful to consider the **source** of a text and its **readership**.

'An unfair exchange' comes from _The Guardian_, a broadsheet newspaper. In one concise sentence, make a generalization about the readership of the newspaper.

Consider Monbiot's intentions. You are now familiar with his article and have found that he is presenting a serious argument to his readers. What is his purpose in writing the article? Ask yourself:

1. Why does he address the reader with the second-person pronoun '_you_'?
2. Does he want to change the thoughts and behaviour of his readers?

Complete the list below with as many points as you possibly can:

The writer, George Monbiot, wants to:
a) inform his readers
b) persuade his readers
c) prick the conscience of his readers

Now, look at 'Side by side in destitution'. However, before you start, here is some information to put the article in context.

CONTEXT

This article was written in December 2001, during America's bombardment of Afghanistan. As it tells you, many thousands of Afghan people fled from their homes. Some managed to enter their neighbouring country, Tajikistan, whilst thousands waited at the border in refugee camps. The situation in Afghanistan was reported in the media at great length, but the people of neighbouring Tajikistan were overlooked. This article tells you about life in Tajikistan following the American bombardment of their neighbour.

Read the article and then, using the dictionary to help you, write down the meaning of the following words and phrases as they are used in the text

Section 1 – 'glean', 'some imagined immorality', 'ravaged', 'human catastrophe zone'
Section 2 – 'vying for power'
Section 3 – 'beleaguered'
Section 4 – 'sphere of influence', 'unmourned'

Now, read the article section by section and write down the answers to the following questions:

Section 1

1. What are Ahmed and Timur's injuries and how are they symbolic of the country's tragedies?
2. Explain the meaning of 'the bitterly opposed factions are as unforgiving as the land'.

Section 2

3. What do the words 'wealth is concentrated in a few not-so-clean hands' tell you about the distribution of money in the country?
4. What have you learned about the lives of children?

Section 3

5. What are the benefits from the war in Afghanistan which some of Tajikistan's people have experienced?

Section 4

6. What hopes does the writer hold for the future of Tajikistan?

You will now have a detailed understanding of the article and are ready to consider the **intentions** of the writer, Olivia Ward.

The **source** of the article is *New Internationalist*, a monthly journal of articles concerning global issues which are often controversial and shocking.

As you did for 'An unfair exchange', ask yourself:

1.   Why does the author use direct speech and **personalize** her very bleak report with named people?
2.   Does the writer want to change the readers' behaviour or opinions?

Make the following list as long as you can:

The writer, Olivia Ward, wants to:
a) inform her readers   c) make her readers feel pity
b) shock her readers

You can now **compare** your lists and notice the ways in which the intentions of the two writers are similar and in which ways they differ. Make two lists headed 'Similarities' and 'Differences' and use your completed lists as a guide for your written answer.

EXAMINER'S
TIP Include detail and brief quotations and make sure that every sentence you write conveys the meaning you intend.

Look at the third part of the assignment:

◆ How effective is the photograph accompanying the introduction to 'The essential guide to cycling holidays'?

EXAMINER'S
TIP When you are asked '**how effective**' a feature is, you are being asked to comment on how successful it is in achieving the purpose – or the effect – which the writer intended for it.

Look at the photograph of the bicycle and the backdrop of Lake Wanaka in New Zealand, and ask yourself what it says to the readers of *Wanderlust*, the travel magazine in which it appears.

Make two columns. In the left-hand one, list the concrete nouns for things shown in the photograph. In the right-hand one, list the abstract nouns which are suggested by the concrete nouns in the left-hand column:

Concrete nouns	Abstract nouns
mountains	freedom
sky	space

Now you can explain what the editor intended the photograph to suggest to a potential reader. Give your own opinion on how successful you think it is.

Finally:

◆ Analyse the writer's aim and language in the introduction to the cycling holidays article.

The text here is the introduction to an article which gives information and advice on planning a cycling holiday abroad. The function of this introductory piece is, therefore, to make the reader think 'Wow! It sounds great! I'd love to do that – tell me more!'. It is the writer's task to make the reader feel this way.

Your analysis of how Lisa Sykes, the writer, achieves this will form your answer to this part of the assignment. You will need to consider:

The informal style

   a)   Colloquial words and expressions, e.g. *'slap in the middle'*
   b)   Vogue or buzz words, e.g. *'you're history'*

> **K E Y**
> **TERM**
>
> **Vogue** or **buzz words** are words and phrases which are currently in fashion.

   c)   Contractions, e.g. *'you're'*, *'it's'*
   d)   The use of the second-person pronoun *'you'*

Find more examples of the features above and explain how they contribute to an informal style, which is appropriate for a travel magazine.

The 'wow!' factor

   e)   Phrasal qualifiers, e.g. *'risk-taking, big jumping mountain bike supremo'*

> **K E Y**
> **TERM**
>
> **Phrasal qualifiers** are phrases used to qualify words.

   f)   Multiple and hyphenated adjectives, e.g. *'huge unmissable flat-topped monolith'*

Find more examples and then explain in writing how your examples of all these different kinds of qualifiers give vigour and pace to the writing.

g) Concrete and proper nouns
Take a paragraph at random and list all the concrete and proper nouns. You will notice that there are very few abstract nouns. Comment on how all the concrete and proper nouns, and the absence of abstract nouns, contribute to the 'muscle' of the writing.

h) Verbs
Verbs can be active or passive. ('You will hear the coyotes' is active; 'The coyotes will be heard' is passive.)
Are most of the verbs in this text active or passive?
Verbs can be in the imperative mood. ('Ignore them' is imperative because it is in command form.)
Find some other examples of imperative verbs.

Now explain how these active and imperative verbs contribute to the energy of the writing.

i) Variation of sentence structure
To create the pace and energy of the 'wow factor', the writer uses varied sentence structure. '*Good brakes and an eye on the next bend and you'll be fine.*' This is a good example of journalistic sentence structure which gives the writing energy, pace, and interest. In this sentence, the clause 'If you have' is understood. This means that even though it does not actually appear, its meaning is understood. This allows the forceful '*Good brakes*' to be fronted, which gives the sentence an emphatic and arresting start: an effective journalistic structure. Uniform sentence structure is generally used for formal, factual writing. Written formally, this sentence would be: 'If you have good brakes and an eye on the next bend, you will be fine.'

Find another example of journalistic sentence structure, and explain its effect.

Now find examples of the following:
◆ A short sentence
◆ A dash followed by a subordinate phrase/clause
◆ A sentence beginning with the connective 'and'

Explain how these sentence structures reinforce the 'wow factor'.

The assignment is now complete.

Saturday, 15 May 1999 The Guardian

Hidden extras

Who else has to pick up the tab when you go on holiday? **George Monbiot** counts the cost of a good time.

An unfair exchange

It's time we introduced a little bit of honesty into the debate about tourism. We don't go abroad to save the planet. We go to enjoy ourselves. Hardly any of the ethical arguments advanced in support of travelling for fun survive even the briefest examination.

Long-distance travel, we are repeatedly told, precipitates a 'cultural exchange'. There's no question that, when we go abroad, we lap up the cultures laid out in front of us, even if what we see is a world away from what is really going on. But what do our hosts obtain from this exchange? If they're lucky, they might get a handful of coins. But apart from discovering what a rude, demanding, dissatisfied lot we can be, it's hard to see how these encounters might offer any real insights into our culture.

We're told that tourism breaks down the barriers between our lives and those of the people we visit. But most tourists remain firmly behind the coach windows, hotel walls and camera lenses that divide them from the countries they travel through. In many parts of the world, tourism has compounded misunderstanding and hostility, especially when residents realise that the next argument – that it brings wealth to local people – is as faulty as all the others.

Tourism makes some people extremely rich, but most of them live in the places from which tourists come, rather than those in which they arrive. Tour companies are adept at ensuring that their customers spend most of their money before they leave, or that the money they spend abroad is swiftly repatriated. Local people are frequently dispossessed of their land and resources as fishing villages give way to hotels, paddy fields are turned into golf courses, and forests are cleared to build airports.

> **Tourism makes some people extremely rich, but most of them live in the places from which tourists come.**

In the slums around Nairobi, Rio, Jakarta and Rangoon live thousands of people whose necessities have made way for our luxuries. No claim is dafter than that tourism helps protect the environment. It is true that it can finance conservation efforts and encourage other countries to preserve the resources they want tourists to see, but few human activities are as destructive as going abroad. Even if we forget the coral reefs smothered in sewage, the savannah woodlands felled for barbeque charcoal and the swamps and streams drained so that we can enjoy showers and flushing toilets, our environmental account would still be firmly in deficit, simply because we have to travel to get there. Air transport is now one of the gravest threats to the global environment, because of the local pollution and disturbance it generates and the vast quantities of carbon dioxide it releases.

Even the oldest argument of all, that travel broadens the mind, collapses when you see what really happens when people go abroad. Tourists, like the customers in old-fashioned shops, are always right. Tour companies try to provide what they expect, rather than showing them what the countries they visit can reasonably provide. For most tourists, the only surprises will be unpleasant ones, when the reality of the countries they visit pricks the bubble in which they travel: thousands return home even more convinced than they were before that foreigners are dirty, deceitful and dangerous.

Tourism is, by and large, an unethical activity, which allows us to have fun at everyone else's expense.

Genuinely low-impact tourism has to take place within the range of boats, trains or bicycles. The money we spend must be spread far more evenly: initiatives that encourage tourists to stay in local people's homes, and which invest in local people's projects, offer the best hope of counteracting some of our negative impacts. Amid the barrage of misleading corporate claims about eco-friendliness, there are one or two companies that have tried to cushion a few of the lesser blows we inflict on the places we visit.

Go, if you have to. But don't pretend you're doing it for anyone other than yourself.

The invisible plight of Afghanistan's neighbour, Tajikistan

Side by side
in destitution

❶ In the seething Green Market of Tajikistan's dusty capital, Dushanbe, two wretched men sit a couple of metres away from each other, trying to glean a bit of shade from the overhanging trees.

Ahmed, an Afghani refugee, is missing a hand: chopped off by the ultra-religious Taliban as punishment for some imagined immorality, before he fled the country two years ago.

Timur, once a Tajik farmer, sits on the pavement, the creases of his ravaged face deepened by the still-powerful autumn sun. He lost a leg to gangrene after being hit by shell fragments during Tajikistan's brutal civil war.

Both men keep their eyes downcast, hoping for handouts from passers by, most of whom are only an economic step above them.

Their plight is symbolic of a region where the bitterly opposed factions are as unforgiving as the land, where even the weather appears to set its face against humankind, and where life is an all-too-brief struggle before the dust settles over exhausted flesh and bones.

Since the US-led bombardment of Afghanistan began, the world's attention has focused on one story of human misery, that of the Afghan people and especially refugees.

At the border, a four-hour drive south, there are many like Ahmed – old, vulnerable and handicapped people stuck in a refugee enclave above a dry river bed, unable to cross into the relative safety of Tajikistan.

But Tajikistan itself is a human catastrophe zone.

❷ Always one of the poorest of the Soviet Union's republics, it slid into destitution after the empire's breakup in 1991, propelled by an explosion of civil war among ethnic, tribal and religious groups vying for power.

Now the war is over. But Tajikistan's 5.7 million people are in a pitched battle for survival. The Government, headed by a Soviet-style leader, Imamali Rakhmonov, has never tackled the republic's endemic corruption, and wealth is concentrated in a few not-so-clean hands.

Most industry has collapsed, and farming has been given over to increasingly unprofitable cotton growing. For the last three years drought has prevented many from feeding themselves from their small plots of land.

The average person earns less than $300 a year, and unemployment is impossible to quantify. Among those who work, salaried jobs are almost non-existent.

'Anyone who has anything to sell tries to sell it,' says Fatloh, a determinedly cheerful woman standing patiently next to an assortment of bright-coloured scarves. 'If you don't sell anything you try to barter. If that doesn't work your kids don't eat.'

Many of the children who earn a pittance at the market carrying heavy sacks on their spindly shoulders have no shoes. Their filthy feet have the sinewy look that comes with chickens past their prime. In the winter some will stay home from school because they lack footwear for the mud and snow.

❸ Not surprisingly, Tajikistan's beleaguered people have greeted the war in Afghanistan with mixed feelings.

On one hand, it's a horrible reminder of their own conflict, which ironically drove thousands of men over the border to hide from victors bent on revenge.

On the other, it's an unexpected opportunity, bringing a steady stream of foreign journalists, aid workers and international officials into a territory that has seen only a few stray back-packers for a decade.

Hotels are suddenly working to capacity, turning away furious would-be customers.

Cafés that catered only to a few regulars are now packing in guests noon and night. Taxi drivers happy to find one or two passengers a day now cruise for hard currency.

But the steadily escalating prices, which spark angry curses from foreigners, are a reminder that Tajikistan's people know in their bones that outsiders give, and they take away.

Over the centuries they have seen few periods of peace and prosperity when their geographical position at the crossroads of Central Asia was a blessing not a curse.

'Everything I earn I put away,' says Mohammed, a taxi driver, apologizing for pocketing a month's wages for a one-day ride. 'I don't need it today, but my family will need it for the winter.'

❹ Humanitarian aid, a necessity for more than one-third of the population, is scarce in obscure Tajikistan, which has been traditionally outside the West's sphere of influence. Now promises are rolling in alongside requests for co-operation in admitting American troops and planes.

But when the war ends, many suspect, the promises may be as empty as the hotels and cafés, and the pockets of the beggars sitting in the dust of the marketplace.

Timur, who once tended his crops and gardens in the arid southern borderland, is expecting no aid from any quarter. As the afternoon wears on he struggles to his one foot with the help of a tree branch that doubles as a cane.

Tonight he may have enough sumoni – the local currency – to buy a round of bread from a fly-blown stand. Or he may not. Either way he will be back again tomorrow until he, too, vanishes like those who came before him, down all the years, unnoticed and unmourned.

Olivia Ward

New Internationalist December 2001

Wanderlust June/July 2001

THE ESSENTIAL GUIDE TO
CYCLING HOLIDAYS

Give the girl a pedal: Lisa Sykes presents the freewheels and the potholes of trips on your bike

Lake Wanaka, South Island, New Zealand (Tony Annis)

❶ My holidays nearly always involve bringing a bike along. Whether you travel independently or pay an operator to organize the whole thing, exploring another country by bike is often the best way. You are more likely to meet the locals – particularly in Asian and African countries, where bicycles are usually the main mode of transport. On a bike you are travelling at the best pace to take in what you are seeing. Flying doesn't give you a hands-on experience, driving is too fast and keeps you on the main roads, while walking simply doesn't cover enough ground. And it's a myth that you need to be super-fit to go on a cycling holiday; the trick is choosing the right trip for you.

❷ The best mountain bike trail I have ever ridden is just behind Highway 89A in Sedona, Arizona. These rolling red paths among the towering mesas of canyon country might be known as Secret Trails, but I'm not exactly giving anything away by revealing their location. Frankly, they must be the worst-kept secret in Sedona because every mountain biker makes a beeline for them. Locals try to put you off by warning that there's no route, no waymarks and hinting that you are bound to get lost. Ignore them, they just want to keep the best riding for themselves.

❸ That said, you will get lost. But not 'stuck in a hot dry desert going round in circles with no hope of finding the trail again' lost. Narrow twisting tracks run in a criss-crossing tangle among the scrub and cacti, but the beauty of Secret Trails is that they are surrounded on three sides by Sedona and on the fourth by Brins Mesa, a huge unmissable flat-topped monolith of striped red rock.

And unlike some other biking hotspots in the Rockies or Canyonlands, you don't have to be a risk-taking, big jumping mountain bike supremo to ride them. Most of the time it's a whoop-de-whoop rollercoaster of a ride – maximum fun for minimal effort and expertise. Just watch out for Devil's Sink, a huge natural hole that the trail runs straight into. Good brakes and an eye on the next bend and you'll be fine. Dodgy brakes and a wandering mind and you're history.

❹ This particular spiderweb of singletrack can keep you occupied for days but there are many other trails to explore; you are slap in the middle of one of the best regions in the world for fun mountain biking. The Wild West location adds spice to the trip; the improbably named Deadman's Pass trail is right below Mescal Mountain, at night you'll hear the coyotes howling from among the Apache ruins and rumour has it that a mountain lion lives in a cave along the old wagon road.

❺ In spring and autumn, the temperature is perfect for shorts and T-shirt riding, though the desert climate makes for colder nights. Sedona has good restaurants, accommodation for whatever budget you're on and it's only two and a half hours from the must-see Grand Canyon – though admittedly by car, not bike.

NON-FICTION INTRODUCTION

A non-fiction text is about something that 'really happened'. It could be from an autobiography written in the first person, like Lorna Sage's description of her school dance on page 49. It could be a hard-hitting opinion piece like Martin Bell's ideas on the role of television in war on page 43. It could recreate the past, like the vivid description of the sport of pig-sticking on page 38. It could be taken from a travel book, a journal, a biography, an autobiography or a memoir. There is a vast world out there and some small part of it will be presented to you.

You will be asked to write about a non-fiction text in the examination. On Paper 1 you will find **non-fiction** examined in Section A. The non-fiction text which you will be given on the examination paper will be an **unseen** one. This means that you will not have been able to read and discuss it beforehand.

The text you will meet in the examination might or might not be related *in theme* to the media texts in your pre-released booklet. Whether it is related in theme or not, it *will* be interesting!

So, you're in the examination hall, and the unseen non-fiction text is in front of you. What should you do?

READING THE TEXT

- Time is precious, so immediately read the question. This means you'll have it in mind as you read the text.
- Read every word at a pace at which you can take in what is happening in the text.
- As you read, underline any lines or phrases which seem important or vivid in any way.
- If you find words you don't know, don't be discouraged and don't waste time worrying about them. Just carry on reading.
- Ideally, you should read the text twice, but this depends on your reading speed.
- If you have read the text at least once carefully, you should be ready to think about answering the question.

WRITING YOUR ANSWER

Some important 'DOs':

- DO make sure every sentence you write answers **relevantly** the question you are being asked
- DO use detail from the text to expand the points you make
- DO use **brief** quotations specifically linked to the points you are making

And some important 'DON'Ts':

- DON'T write out the question – you will only waste time
- DON'T write an introduction in which you say what you're going to do – just do it!
- DON'T quote at length – long quotations become just copying out and won't earn you any credit
- DON'T leave out any part of the question

You won't know, of course, exactly what you will be asked about the text in the examination, but you will need to be able to explain:

- **the content of the text**
- **the writer's purpose**
- **the effect of the writer's use of language**

CHECKLIST

The following is a useful checklist. You will meet these topics and terms as you work through the non-fiction assignments in this book. When you have finished the assignments, it would be helpful to go through this list to make sure you understand them and can use them in your writing.

Content and purpose

- Description of emotions or place
  Is this intended to: move the reader, recreate the past?
- Argument and opinion
  Is this intended to: inform, persuade, change the reader's opinion?
- Narrative account
  Is this intended to: entertain, shock, involve, move the reader?

Language used for effect

- Imagery (e.g. metaphors, similes, alliteration, personification) – how is it used?
- Modifiers (adjectives, adverbs) – are they single, multiple or hyphenated?

- Technical or specialist vocabulary – how is it used?
- Verbs – are they active, passive, imperative?
- Word length – are words short/long; monosyllabic/polysyllabic?
- Nouns – are they concrete, abstract, proper?

Organization

- Sentences – are they short/long for effect? Do they use subordinate clauses?
- Punctuation – are there parenthetical commas, semi-colons, exclamation marks, continuation dots, question marks, quotation marks, dashes?
- Paragraphs – are they short/long? What is the position of the topic sentence?
- Connectives – are these words and phrases used to mark textual stages?
- Are introductory and concluding sentences/paragraphs used effectively?
- Is chronological sequencing indicated by verb tenses, including the conditional and past and present continuous?

Interpretation

- What mood/tone is created by language effects, e.g. reflective, lively, humorous, emotional?
- What connotations/associations are linked with the words used?
- What narrative voice is used: first person (I); second person (you); third person (he, she, it, they)?
- What use is made of dialogue – direct speech, indirect speech, internal dialogue used to convey mood/character/argument/narrative?
- Is use made of humour and irony?

NON-FICTION UNIT 1

ASSIGNMENT

- Explain the arrangement which the writer made with the men who caught the birds.
- Explain the dangers involved in pig-sticking.
- Explore in detail how the two writers achieve different effects through their use of language.

The texts for this assignment are on pages 37–38.

The first two bullet points in the assignment are asking you to **select** the appropriate 'bits' from these two texts in order to answer the questions **relevantly**.

Look at the first one:

- Explain the arrangement which the writer made with the men who caught the birds.

First of all, you need to understand the text. Read 'Buying birds of paradise' through and then write down the definitions of the following words and phrases as they are used in the text. Use a dictionary to help you.

Paragraph 1: '*ventured*'
Paragraph 2: '*no ulterior designs*'
Paragraph 3: '*half-putrefied*', '*defiled*', '*plumage*', '*perceptibly differ*'

EXAMINER'S TIP

The word '**barter**' (noun and verb) does not appear in the text, but understanding its meaning will help you understand and explain the arrangement the men made. Look it up in the dictionary.

Read through the text again and **select** the information which is relevant to the arrangement the men made. Write your explanation **concisely** and clearly.

Now, look at the second part of the assignment:

- Explain the dangers involved in pig-sticking.

Read the text carefully. To help you understand what the text is about, write a two-sentence summary of each of the three paragraphs.

Now read through the text again. This time, as you read the text, focus on the following four sources of danger. If you have your own copy of the text, highlight the lines that tell you about the dangers involved. (Do <u>not</u> write in the book.)

a)   The spear   c)   The horses
b)   The boar   d)   Hunting alone

EXAMINER'S TIP If you use a different colour for each source of danger, you will find it easier to write your answer.

When you have explained each source of danger, you have finished this part of the assignment.

Now for the most challenging part of the assignment:

◆ Explore in detail how the two writers achieve different effects through their use of language.

KEY TERM First of all, you need to know exactly what 'effects' means. A piece of writing has an 'effect' on you, the reader. If it makes you laugh, it has a **humorous effect**. If it makes your eyes tingle with tears, it has a **sad** or **melancholy effect**. If it lifts your spirits and makes you feel cheerful, it has a **happy** or **uplifting effect**. You can probably think of some more examples. Of course, a piece of writing can convey more than one effect. It then conveys **different** or **various effects**.

Now, you are ready to consider these two texts. Make a column for 'Buying birds of paradise' and another for 'Pig-sticking in India'. Write down all the **effects** of the texts you can think of. The list has been started for you:

<u>Buying birds</u>   <u>Pig-sticking</u>
factual   lively
unemotional   emotional

When you have finished your list, write a sentence which summarizes the main difference between the effects in the two texts. You could write:

'Pig-sticking in India' has a livelier and more dramatic effect than 'Buying birds of paradise', which has a more formal and unemotional effect.

Now you can start on the difficult part, which is **explaining** how the different effects are achieved through the writers' **use of language**. How does the writers' choice of words, phrases, punctuation, sentence and paragraph structure achieve these effects?

The first **language feature** you will focus on is the **structure of sentences and paragraphs** in 'Buying birds of paradise'.

EXAMINER'S
TIP
It might be helpful to remember that this text was written more than one hundred years ago.

Work your way through the following, writing down your answers:

1. How many semi-colons are there?
2. What does a semi-colon do to the length of a sentence?
3. What effect do long sentences have on a text?
4. How many words are there in the longest and shortest sentences?
5. How many main and subordinate clauses are there in the longest sentence?
6. What is the average number of words in the sentences in this text?
7. Is there any variety to the sentence structure?
8. Find the connecting words and phrases at the beginning of the paragraphs.
9. How do they help to shape the writer's narrative account?
10. How do they add to the formal effect of the writing?

Now, focus on the **structure of sentences and paragraphs** in 'Pig-sticking in India'. Work through the following, writing down your answers as you did for the other text:

1. Find the shortest and the longest sentences.
2. How different in length are they?
3. Find all the lines of direct speech.
4. How do they contribute to your enjoyment of the passage?
5. How do they contribute to the lively effect of the text?
6. Find the exclamation marks.
7. What is their effect? How do they add to the drama of the text?
8. What is the effect of the dash?
9. How does the writer use topic sentences in his paragraphs?
10. How do they help guide the reader?

You are now ready to write up your answer on how the sentence and paragraph structure of the two writers achieves different effects. Use your answers to the questions above in your response. You could begin:

The writer of 'Buying birds of paradise' uses long sentences with a subordinate clause or a second main clause linked to the main clause with a semi-colon. This sentence structure is formal and old-fashioned, and it is repeated all the way through. This conveys an effect of self-control and organization in the writer. The average length of the sentences is . . .

The second **language feature** is the use of **nouns, verbs,** and **adjectives** in 'Buying birds of paradise'. Work through the following, writing down your answers:

1. Find the nouns in the first paragraph.
2. How many of them are **modified** (described) by adjectives?
3. Are the nouns mostly **concrete** (names of things you could touch) or **abstract** (names of concepts or qualities)?
4. What effect does this create?
5. Find the verbs in the second paragraph.
6. What do these verbs convey? Actions? Thoughts?
7. How do they help to make the text factual?
8. How does the reported speech in the second paragraph contribute to the overall effect of the text?

Do the same for the **nouns, verbs** and **adjectives** in 'Pig-sticking':

1. Find the nouns and the adjectives.
2. Are the nouns mostly concrete or abstract? What effect does this have on the writing?
3. Why do you think the writer uses so many adjectives?
4. How do the nouns and adjectives contribute to the overall effect of the passage?
5. How many verbs expressing movement can you find?
6. How do they contribute to the passage's drama and liveliness?

Again, write a complete answer, using your answers to these questions to provide evidence and detail. You could begin:

The writer of 'Pig-sticking in India' uses a great number of concrete nouns, which are frequently qualified by one or two adjectives - 'heavy lead weight'; 'flat alluvial plain'. These concrete nouns appeal to the senses. This makes the scene lively and it creates a vivid picture in the reader's mind . . .

When you have finished, you have completed the whole assignment.

Buying birds of paradise in Waigion, New Guinea in 1869

1 My first business was to send for the men who were accustomed to catch the birds of paradise. Several came, and I showed them my hatchets, beads, knives, and handkerchiefs; and explained to them as well as I could by signs, the price I would give for fresh-killed specimens. It is the universal custom to pay for everything in advance; but only one man ventured on this occasion to take goods to the value of two birds. The rest were suspicious, and wanted to see the result of the first bargain with the strange white man, the only one who had ever come to their island.

2 After three days, my man brought me the first bird – a very fine specimen, and alive, but tied up in a small bag, and consequently its tail and wing feathers very much crushed and injured. I tried to explain to him, and to the others that came with him, that I wanted them as perfect as possible, and that they should either kill them, or keep them on a perch with a string to their leg. As they were now apparently satisfied that all was fair, and that I had no ulterior designs upon them, six others took away goods; some for one bird, some for more; and one for as many as six. They said they had to go a long way for them, and that they would come back as soon as they caught any.

3 At intervals of a few days or a week, some of them would return bringing me one or more birds; but though they did not bring any more in bags, there was not much improvement in their condition. As they caught them a long way off in the forest, they would scarcely ever come with one, but would tie it by the leg to a stick, and put it in their house till they caught another. The poor creature would make violent efforts to escape, would get among the ashes, or hang suspended by the leg till the limb was swollen and half-putrefied, and sometimes die of starvation and worry. One had its beautiful head all defiled by pitch from a dammar torch; another had been so long dead that its stomach was turning green. Luckily, however, the skin and plumage of these birds is so firm and strong, that they bear washing and cleaning better than almost any other sort; and I was generally able to clean them so well that they did not perceptibly differ from those I had shot myself.

Pig-sticking in India in the 1920s

1 Some rated pig-sticking as 'the most dangerous sport of all. You can't see the country you're riding over because the long grass hides where you are going, and you have to go at a gallop to keep up with the boar. The horse may put its foot in a hole or a hollow and turn a somersault, and the spear itself is also a danger because of the heavy lead weight at its base.' John Rivett-Carnac recalls an instance of a rider who dropped his spear: 'The lead butt went forward, the point entered the horse's chest and came out behind his saddle, just missing the rider.' The boar itself was a formidable quarry: 'I had several horses cut and on one occasion a big boar charged me on and got right through my riding-boot. The tusk broke off in the bones of my instep and made quite a nasty wound. I had my boot cut off, disinfected the wound, then tied the boot on again and went on pig-sticking – which shows how keen we were in those days.'

2 The first rule of pig-sticking was never to do it alone. John Rivett-Carnac had a friend who broke the rule: 'The boar got him and stood over him and went on cutting his back as he lay with his arms along his sides. He was cut to bits and had to have over a hundred stitches in his back.' In more orthodox situations 'hog hunters' armed with 'hog-spears' rode in groups of four. 'It was cruel sport,' admits Raymond Vernede, 'but the boar is a very valiant animal and he very often got away. When he died he died gamely, charging you, and this was why it was so important to have a really sharp spear to finish him off quickly. I can remember being charged by a pig head-on and getting my spear stuck in the front of his head, and as we passed each other I was carried clean out of the saddle and ended up sitting on the ground still holding the butt of the spear with the pig in front of me stone dead.'

3 Pig-sticking meets were held in the cold weather 'when the crops had all been cut and the land was fairly bare'. The largest of these meets was on the flat alluvial plain of the Ganges near Meerut, when teams and individuals competed for the Kadir Cup: 'One of the sights of dawn, just before starting the first beat, was that regular sight of all the chaps standing round holding their spears up and sharpening the blades to razor sharp with a small stone. Immediately a pig broke the horseman nearest the pig was traditionally the first on and would normally have the first chance of spearing it. The first spear got alongside the pig and tried to make it charge him. This was the moment you waited for. You held the spear under your arm in the traditional tent-pegging manner and you depended on the pig charging to drive your spear into the shoulder of the pig. If you didn't get the pig on to the point of your spear and it grazed off, of course the pig could cut your horse terribly.' Not everybody took to pig-sticking. 'I was persuaded to go out pig-sticking one Sunday morning' recalls John Morris, 'on a horse which was lent to me by someone I'd never met in my life. While we were waiting in a sort of thicket for the pigs to break out the Master saw me on this rather restive white horse and shouted at me in a rather offensive way: "Take that bloody horse under cover!" When the pig finally appeared the horse I was on simply shot away like a streak of lightning. It had a mouth like iron and I was totally unable to control it, but I managed to stick on to it somehow or other until we arrived at its stable, by which time I'd lost all interest in pig-sticking and never indulged in it again!'

"Whoof whoof."
A clever old horse taking care of a novice

NON-FICTION UNIT 2

ASSIGNMENT

◆ Explain Martin Bell's argument about television news coverage of war.
◆ How does Martin Bell's use of language strengthen his argument?

The text for this assignment is on page 43.

CONTEXT

Before you begin to read the text, you need the following background information:
◆ Martin Bell is writing about the role of television reporting during the war in Bosnia (1992–1995), where he was a war reporter.
◆ At the time he is writing about, the Muslims, Croats and Serbs were rival groups involved in the civil war in Bosnia.
◆ Sarajevo is the capital of Bosnia. Santici, Vitez and Ahmici are other towns in Bosnia.
◆ The Old Kent Road is in London.
◆ Elie Wiesel was a Jewish writer who survived the Second World War Nazi concentration camps.

Before you can begin to trace Martin Bell's argument, you must have a thorough understanding of the text. Read it through once, carefully. Then go through it again, writing down your answers to the following questions. Use brief quotations from the text in your answers.

Paragraph 1

1. Why had Bell taken so few of the images himself?
2. Who was Kresimir and why did he do the work that he did?

Paragraph 2

3. What kind of images were filmed?
4. Why did Bell go back to the Old Kent Road?

Paragraph 3

5. What are '*bang bang*' images?
6. How does Bell illustrate '*bang bang*' images?

Paragraph 4

7. Why were Kresimir's images edited?
8. In what ways does Bell feel that the editing affected the reporting of war?

Paragraph 5

    9. What does Bell feel was missing from these reports?
  10. Why does he criticize the BBC?
  11. In what way was the war being '*prettified*'?

Paragraph 6

  12. What does Bell feel happens to '*reality*' when it is transmitted through a television report?
  13. What does Bell feel can never be transmitted?

Paragraph 7

  14. Why does Bell himself feel the need to censor some pictures?
  15. Why does he refer to Elie Wiesel?

Paragraph 8

  16. What does Bell feel have been the failures of television reporting of the war in Bosnia?

Having worked through the text in this way, you are now ready to consider the first part of the assignment:

◆ Explain Martin Bell's argument about television news coverage of war.

Your answers to the questions above, along with your selected quotations, will be the basis for your answer. You will need to **select** relevant points and quotations from what you have already written. Remember to put quotation marks around the words you quote from the text, and keep them **pithy**. This means that they should be brief and to the point.

To give your answer structure, write in paragraphs. Make sure that you link everything you write to Bell's argument. In this way you will keep your answer **relevant** and **focused**.

Use the following headings as topics for each of your paragraphs:

a)   The value of '*bang bang*' images
b)   The '*good taste guidelines*'
c)   What edited images convey
d)   The sanitizing and prettifying of war
e)   Television and illusion
f)   What television can never portray
g)   Bell's self-censorship of images
h)   Bell's conclusion

You have now finished the first part of the assignment and are ready for the second part:

◆ How does Martin Bell's use of language strengthen his argument?

When a writer presents an argument, what does he or she want you, the reader, to do and feel? Consider the following list and add to it if you can:

The writer's aims are to make me, the reader:
a) read
b) think
c) get involved
d) be persuaded
e) be convinced
f) respect him or her
g) believe him or her
h) trust him or her

So how does Martin Bell do it?
To give your response structure, work under the following headings:

Choice of words

How does Bell's **choice of words** help him to convince you, and to achieve the other aims in the list above?

In the first paragraph, Bell tells us that he didn't film all the war footage himself:

'To be honest, we did very little of this for ourselves...'

He introduces, or prefaces, the fact with the phrase 'To be honest'.
1. What kind of relationship does this phrase establish between reader and writer?
2. If Bell had followed the phrase with an obvious exaggeration or untruth, what difference would it have made to that relationship?

Write down your answers to these questions.

Bell uses some specialist vocabulary to describe his work: 'images', 'bang bang', 'rushes'.
3. What effect do these specialist terms have on the relationship between you as reader and the writer?
4. How do they contribute to the power of Bell's argument?

Write down your answers to these questions.

Find two more examples of words and phrases in the text which you think are relevant to the 'aims list' above. Analyse them in a similar way as these examples.

Sentence structure

In paragraphs 7 and 8, Bell uses continuation dots. He first uses them when he quotes Elie Wiesel and secondly when he is explaining that he cannot show some images of war on television:

> 'I cannot say ... I cannot say them'
> 'We cannot show . . . we cannot show them'

1. What is the effect of Bell's echoing of Elie Wiesel's words?
2. What feelings in Bell do the continuation dots convey?
3. How do these feelings affect the relationship between reader and writer?

Write down your answers to these questions.

Now find examples of three other features of sentence structure in the text to analyse in a similar way.

Features to look for include the effective use of:
a) questions
b) brackets
c) semi-colons
d) parenthetical commas
e) sentences of contrasting length

You have now finished analysing how Martin Bell's choice of words and sentence structure strengthen his argument, and have completed the assignment.

WAR IS A BAD TASTE BUSINESS *by Martin Bell*

1 It was January 1994, at the height of the fighting between Muslims and Croats in the Lasva valley, and we had access to the most extraordinary images of front-line combat that I have ever seen. To be honest, we did very little of this for ourselves (I had perhaps become over-cautious since my collision with the mortar fragments). It was done for us by Kresimir, a gentle soul and professional musician who carried a camera on our behalf, though he would accept no payment. His motive was that he wanted the world to know what was happening to his people. He was a Croat trusted by the HVO's front-line commander Tihomir Blaskic, the soldiers in the trenches were his friends, and he went where they went.

2 The result was a series of images of raw power and great impact: winter warfare in a First World War landscape of barbed wire and trenches and bunkers, an advancing infantryman hit and killed in the snow under the eye of the camera, and street fighting in the ruins of Santici with the Croats winching out their casualties under fire. Kresimir was also lucky to be alive. In Santici he was hit by an AK47 bullet at a hundred yards, but it struck him on the front plate of the flak jacket we had given him only the week before. (Much later, I took the damaged ceramic plate to the RBR Armour Company in the Old Kent Road, where these things are made by an entirely Ghanaian labour force. I was led down to the factory floor, work stopped for a moment, and in a heartfelt but inadequate speech I thanked them for saving his life.)

3 His pictures were the very model of what is known in the trade as 'bang bang': so close to the action, indeed part of the action, that no news editor would think of dropping them from his programme. But in their raw form, the 'rushes', they showed the costs as well as the courage that this kind of combat exacts. As the Croats advanced, they recaptured a house where a dozen of their comrades in arms had been surprised and their position overrun in the first assault, then apparently tortured and executed: their bodies were found stacked in a room and bound together with wire. Kresimir's coverage showed that too, and the grief of the mothers and wives in Vitez when they found their worst fears confirmed.

4 These images also fell foul of the 'good taste guidelines': even mourning was put out of bounds. The reports still ran, of course – thanks to Kresimir, they were too vivid not to. But all that was left in them was the 'bang bang', apparently heroic pictures of camouflage-clad figures blazing away amid the ruins; and even the ruins seemed picturesque, being sunlit at this season against the snow. It was about as close to reality as a Hollywood action movie. Indeed at times fact imitated fiction: one of the Croats' warlords, Darko Kraljevic, would dash out of cover and fire both his weapons on the move, revolver in one hand and sub-machine gun in the other, in the manner of Arnold Schwarzenegger terminating something.

5 What was missing in all this, and in our reports of it, was a sense of the human price being paid, the irredeemable waste of young lives. I am a fierce BBC loyalist; it is an institution that it is easy to be proud of even today, and a force for truth and freedom in the world; also, at the personal level, I am fortunate to have worked throughout my career for caring and decent people, and I bite the hand that feeds me very seldom. But it did seem to me and still does that in this case, in our anxiety not to offend and upset people, we were not only sanitizing war but even prettifying it, as if it were an acceptable way of settling disputes, and its victims never bled to death but rather expired gracefully out of sight. How tactful of them, I thought. But war is real and war is terrible. War is a bad taste business.

6 Television by its very nature has an aptitude for illusion anyway. Reality is somehow diminished by being framed in the modest rectangle in the corner of the living room. Images from the front line especially lose something in the transfer, and take on the quality almost of travelogue, as if in a scene from one of P. J. O'Rourke's *Holidays in Hell*. So often in the course of this war, harried by the ever-imminent deadline, I would rush from battlefield to cutting room – often a journey of only a few hundred yards – clutching my field cassettes with a survivor's pride and eager to get at them. Then, having viewed them, I would ask myself, is that really all there was? Was that it? Something was missing, something that will always be missing in the compressed world of the tube: the sense of the surrounding reality, the sharper perceptions of the eye as against the camera, the sights and sounds and smells of actually being there. For this there is no video substitute, not even the 'virtual reality' of TV news.

7 And yes, we do self-censor. Even those of us who resist the external censorship of real-life violence find images that we have to leave, as we used to say, on the cutting-room floor. Nearly all the TV pictures of the mortar bombing of the market place in Sarajevo – indeed of all that city's mass killings – seemed to me to fall within this category. So did the scenes in the cellar in Ahmici where a Muslim family of seven, including mother, grandparents and small children, were burned to death by the Croats. In the end I used a single picture, a close-up of a burned hand, as emblematic of the rest, and even that was hard to include though necessary. I have become, I suppose, more hardened than most to man's inhumanity to man – or, at least, less surprised by it. But when in that setting I tried to utter a few words to the camera (as in most reports from far-flung places we are expected to) I found that for the first time in my life the words would not come out. Horror paralysed thought. I was reminded of Elie Wiesel who said of some events that he had witnessed, 'There are things I cannot say … I cannot say them.'

8 In the same way there are things we cannot show … we cannot show them. And others that lie beyond the range of our cameras. Television often stands accused, at least in the military circles in which I move, of exaggerating the events it relates and wrenching them out of context, but in Bosnia it has consistently understated the facts where it did know them and under-reported them where it didn't.

NON-FICTION UNIT 3

ASSIGNMENT

- Explain how Lorna Sage's dancing partner differed in reality and in her imagination.
- How does the writer's use of language help to create the vividness of her description in the extract?

The text for this assignment is on page 49.

Before tackling the assignment, you need to be sure that you have a detailed understanding of the text. So, read 'The school dance' carefully. Now, go through it again, and write down your answers to the following questions as you read:

Paragraph 1

1. In what ways did the dress imagined by Lorna and the dress imagined by her mother contrast with the dress that she actually wore?

Paragraph 2

2. What did Lorna feel before and after the first dance with her partner?

Paragraph 3

3. What was so '*awful*' about the second dance with him?

Paragraph 4

4. Why is Lorna not impressed by what she finds out about the identity of her partner?

Paragraph 5

5. How do Gail's experience, Lorna's last waltz, and her lift home contribute to her feelings at the end of the evening?

Now you are ready to answer the first part of the assignment:

- Explain how Lorna Sage's dancing partner differed in reality and in her imagination.

Explaining what was going on in Lorna's imagination will be more difficult than explaining the reality of her partner. You need to do a little work first.

Lorna was a studious girl and very much influenced by the literature she had read. You need to understand the significance of the following phrases. You will probably need to ask questions or use a reference book to explain them fully:

> 'My imagined cavalier'
> 'The prince of ennui'
> 'As unobtainable as a sonneteer's mistress'

Now, back to the assignment title. It would be helpful to make two columns headed Reality and Imagination. Read through the text again and, underneath each heading, write down appropriate quotations and explanations as you go. Your answers to all the previous questions will help you.

You could start like this:

Reality	Imagination
Her partner stank of beer 'like the open maws of the pub cellars'	The evening's 'true, occult ritual' hadn't started
He was 'distracted, disjointed and clammy' – totally unattractive	Lorna was waiting for something magical and out of this world to happen; some kind
He couldn't dance properly; he was sweaty and didn't talk to her	of rite of passage ceremony to take place.

When you have completed your columns, you can write up your answer to this part of the assignment. Use **brief** quotations.

Now you are ready for the second part of the assignment:

◆ How does the writer's use of language help to create the vividness of her description in the extract?

You are no longer focusing on just Lorna and her dancing partner. Now you are looking at the whole text. It certainly does give a vivid impression of the occasion, and of Lorna's feelings. How does the writer do it?

The writer's varied sentence structure

Take this sentence, for example:

> 'This time, instead of counting, he talked as we jogged around the floor, into my ear, in a whispered shout over the music: his mother had broken her arm falling from a stepladder in the shop where she worked, where she wouldn't have to work if her sons and her husband looked after her properly, which they didn't, his own bad behaviour was adding to her troubles, no wonder he was pissed …'

The writer is describing how her partner Victor was talking as they danced. The first part of the sentence up to the colon tells you that. The sentence could have ended there with a full stop, but the writer chooses to use a colon and continue the sentence. Why?

The writer continues the sentence with five **clauses** which are not linked with **connectives**. This informal sentence structure conveys the torrent of disorganized speech that pours from Victor. This conveys in a vivid way Victor's slight drunkenness and it also gives the reader an impression of the barrage of complaints which Victor hears from his mother about her sons and husband.

The final clause 'no wonder he was pissed …' is not linked with a connective to the previous clause and the reader must make the jump to Lorna's own reaction to Victor's flow of speech about his family. She understands why he might get drunk to escape them. The **continuation dots** are used to suggest further Lorna's feeling of being bombarded by the 'whispered shout' of words, the music and the occasion. For the moment, she has no organized reply.

For your own response to this part of the assignment, look for another example of a complex sentence and analyse it in the same way, showing how the writer's choice of sentence structure adds to the vividness of the extract.

Find some further features of sentence structure and analyse them in the same way.

Look, for example, for the effective use of:
a) a short sentence
b) brackets
c) parenthetical dashes
d) italics
e) questions
f) quotation marks

The writer's vocabulary

You have already established that there is a contrast between what Lorna dreams about, and the reality. Now look at how this contrast is conveyed through the writer's choice of vocabulary.

In paragraph 4, Lorna explains Victor's background. List some words which are used to describe his ordinary, unglamorous background. Start this way:

a) 'Council estate'
b) 'Drapers'

When the writer describes her longing to escape this ordinary background, her vocabulary becomes more complex. List the words and phrases used to describe Lorna's dream suitor. Start this way:

a) 'magical mentor'
b) 'prince of ennui'

You can see that the two lists are very different kinds of words. Write down the dictionary definitions for the following words. They will help you in your next task:
a) idealized
b) romanticized
c) glamorized
d) mundane
e) sophisticated

Now, write a detailed explanation of how the writer's words vividly convey the division between reality and dream in the text.

The writer's imagery

Sometimes, as in this case, it is helpful to note language features that a writer chooses **not** to use. Did you notice how many metaphors and similes the writer uses in this text? One simile describes Gail's dancing partner as '*like a startled gazelle*', but you will probably not find much more metaphorical language. How does this non-metaphorical language add to the vividness of the description?

If the writer is not using similes and metaphors for effect, what is she using?
Complete this list with seven more nouns modified with adjectives:

a) 'new-fangled, stinging deodorants'
b) 'gap-toothed grimace'
c) 'black, black hair'

Have you found mainly abstract or concrete nouns? What effect does this have?
What is the effect of multiple and hyphenated adjectives?

Now, find further examples of alliteration:

a) 'Snickered sarcastically'
b) 'Messy mark'

Write a paragraph on how the writer's choice of adjectives, alliteration, and non-metaphorical language contributes to the vividness of the text.

You have now written about how the writer's sentence structure, vocabulary, and imagery help to create the vividness of the description in the text. You have completed the assignment.

THE SCHOOL DANCE *by Lorna Sage*

1 On the day itself we were allowed to go home in the afternoon to get ready. My mother and I had compromised over my new dress – her visions of me in floating white chiffon which anyway we couldn't afford, and mine of something cheap in all senses, off the shoulder and tight in the skirt, with a lot of dark red about it, which I'd seen in the catalogue, had converged on a princess-line calf-length frock 'that emphasizes your pretty figure' mused the Shrewsbury saleswoman, looking over my shoulder, smoothing it down over my hips for just a little too long. It was Wedgwood blue, with a white pattern and a square nearly low neck, and I secretly liked it, although I complained it was babyish. Then back to school, to the hot, heaped-up 'cloakroom' and a confused smell of forbidden scent, bath salts, talc, hairspray and new-fangled, stinging deodorants, and familiar people transformed with shiny sandals and flushed faces jostling for the one full-length mirror. I thought I'd faint when we got into the gym, the ceiling seemed to have vanished, the room stretched upwards into space, and there were pools of solid-looking darkness on the floor and in the corners.

2 The awful business of beginning fell to the head boy and head girl, but at least they didn't have to choose, or be chosen. What if no one asked you? You'd gradually sink into oblivion and the dark would close over your head. Boys sidled across the hall, their temples glistening with sweat and Brylcreem, nudging and shoving each other, and suddenly here was one, saying 'May I ...' Well, yes, the relief was enormous and this was easy, a waltz. Once my first pang of gratitude had subsided, I noticed that my partner was preoccupied too. He seemed to be having trouble remembering the steps, for he was pumping my arm and counting under his breath (one, two, three), and his breath smelled like the open maws of the pub cellars that gaped on Whitchurch pavements on delivery day. Beer. He'd been drinking and, although in theory this was glamorous because forbidden (and he was anyway certainly under age), in fact he was distracted, disjointed and clammy. He stepped on my feet (one, two ...) and groaned as if his pain was greater than mine, and then it was over and I was back in my corner, my white shoes a bit scuffed, still waiting for the evening's true, occult ritual to start.

3 Now one of the scatter of sixth-formers wearing dinner jackets would surely pick me out, someone older (teachers only danced with teachers, alas) whose casual touch would unlock the mysteries of the quickstep and A-level physics. But my next two partners seemed just as inept and nervous as me. I wasn't getting anywhere and, as if to rub it in, my first partner was back, more dishevelled than before, his collar unbuttoned, mopping his brow. This time, instead of counting, he talked as we jogged around the floor, into my ear, in a whispered shout over the music: his mother had broken her arm falling from a stepladder in the shop where she worked, where she wouldn't have to work if her sons and her husband looked after her properly, which they didn't, his own bad behaviour was adding to her troubles, no wonder he was pissed ...

He snickered sarcastically and seemed about to burst into tears. This was awful. Each dance with him took me further from my imagined cavalier, he was leaving his messy mark on me – this time it wasn't just the bruised toes and the dirty shoes, there was definitely a damp patch on my dress in the small of my back where his hand had been and my hair felt sticky where he'd leaned on me to tell his story. Who was he? How could I get rid of him?

4 Back in the girls' corner, they knew who he was at least, he was a distant cousin of one of the fifth-formers, a gangling pariah called Sheila who had wildly protruding teeth and had once tried to befriend me when I was a pariah with braces. He was Victor Sage, his mother's pride but no one else's, well known for clowning, drinking and fighting after hours behind the Back Street Vaults, and they lived in Whitchurch on the council estate and his mother worked in Dudleston's, the drapers on High Street. My head was starting to ache. I went and stared at myself in the mirror in the 'Ladies'. Of course. That was where my mother had worked before the war, with Gladys, who must be his mother. I recalled mutual boasting sessions, once in particular when I'd passed the Scholarship, and so had Victor said his mother proudly to mine, pretending to wrap up some lingerie to borrow time to talk. In fact, my mother had often stopped off to talk to Mrs Sage as she now was, while I kicked my heels and tugged at her sleeve. My tormentor was essence of Whitchurch, then, part of the familiar tangle I so yearned to slough off. And he wasn't handsome either, with that gap-toothed grimace, although that wouldn't have mattered if he'd been the magical mentor I'd looked forward to, the prince of ennui.

5 My friend Gail had done much better when it came to realizing her imaginings. Her eyes shone and she hummed a few bars of Paul Anka's number one hit, 'Diana', about a mythical older woman, which was written when he was fourteen and inspired by falling in love with his babysitter. Against all the odds she'd discovered in Whitchurch a Paul Anka lookalike – same high cheekbones and black, black hair – and although this one's eyes were blue and Paul's were brown (he was 'of Syrian extraction'), they were deep-set and inward-looking in just the right way. He was called Michael Price, a boy like a startled gazelle who refused to dance at all; he was probably as unobtainable as a sonneteer's mistress and that was as it should be. For my part I returned to the floor furious. The deputy head boy asked me to dance, but by now it was too late. When Vic Sage reappeared, as I knew he would, I lost my temper, forgot I was shy, and told him to *go away*. He was shocked and staggered back on his heels for a moment, but it was no good, the last waltz was upon us and there was no time to wait for another partner. So we trudged around the gym one final time in silence, and then I bundled on my coat in the cloakroom, my punctual father in full view of everyone picked me up outside in a cattle truck (the car had broken down again) and my mortification was complete.

POETRY INTRODUCTION

When you study the varied poems in this section, you will be looking at '**Poetry from Different Cultures and Traditions**'. Spanning no less than thirteen hundred years, they give you insight into places as different as the weed-locked inland sea of Japan and a war-damaged Bosnian city, and take you to places as distant and varied as the Caribbean and Australia.

You will study 'Poetry from Different Cultures and Traditions' for your examination. The poems will be in your **pre-released booklet** and on your examination paper.

The pre-released booklet will contain 8–10 poems. You will have it in the January before the summer examination, so you will have plenty of time in class to study and write about the poems. When you sit the examination, you will therefore already be familiar with them all.

Starting with the examination in 2005, you will not be allowed to write any notes or comments on your pre-released booklet.

You will be asked to write about the poetry in Section A on Paper 2. The question will have several bullet points which will ask you to write about a named poem in the pre-released booklet and, **in addition**, an **unseen** poem on the examination paper. Although you will be familiar with the named poem in the pre-released booklet, the unseen poem will be new to you and you will not have been able to read it or discuss it.

So, you're in the examination hall, and the poetry question and the unseen poem are in front of you. What should you do?

READING THE POEMS

Read the question straight away. This means that you will have it in mind as you read the poems. You will probably be asked to compare the two poems in some way, but **the focus of your detailed analysis will be on the unseen poem**.

Read the unseen poem twice, slowly. Then refresh your memory of the named pre-released poem.

WRITING YOUR ANSWER

Some important 'DOs':

◆ DO use **brief** quotations selected to illustrate the point you are making
◆ DO make sure every sentence you write is **relevant** to what you are being asked
◆ DO comment on the cultural distinctiveness evident in the poems
◆ DO **analyse** meaning and language

And some important 'DON'Ts':

◆ DON'T just narrate or describe the content of the poems
◆ DON'T quote at length
◆ DON'T waste words – be focused and economical!
◆ DON'T leave out any of the bullet points in the question

CHECKLIST

The following is a useful checklist. You will meet these topics and terms as you work through the poetry assignments in this book. When you have finished the assignments, it would be helpful to go through the list again to make sure you understand the points and can use them in your writing.

Cultural distinctiveness

◆ What is the geographical setting and the climate of the poem?
◆ What attitudes and feelings are shown, e.g. towards death or marriage?
◆ Daily lives and routines – how are they shown?
◆ Customs and traditions – are they shown in the poem?
◆ Language – is there any culturally specific vocabulary?

Structure

Are the following used? If so, how and why?

◆ Verses/stanzas
◆ Rhyme schemes
◆ Rhyming couplets
◆ Stressed and unstressed syllables
◆ Enjambment
◆ End-stopped lines
◆ Poetic sentence structure, e.g. verbless sentences, non-standard punctuation

Language used for effect

Are the following features used? If so, how and why?

- Metaphors and similes
- Alliteration
- Personification
- Modifiers (adjectives, adverbs) – in lists, or hyphenated
- Monosyllabic (one-syllable) words or polysyllabic (longer) words
- Hard and soft consonants; long and short vowels used for their sound effects
- Different types of nouns – archaic, culturally specific, proper, lists of nouns

Interpretation

- Are there elements in the poem that are specific to a particular culture?
- How is mood/tone created by language effects?
- What are the associations/connotations/'colours' of words?
- Metaphorical language – how is it used?
- Does the poem contain irony and humour?
- Think about the poem titles.

POETRY UNIT 1

ASSIGNMENT

The texts for this assignment are on pages 57–58.

- Explain the *literal meanings* and then the '*weighty truths*' of the three poems.
- Show how the words and verse structures give the creatures in the poems their own individual characters.

CONTEXT

These poems are based on the **fables** of Aesop, who was born in ancient Greece in 572 BC. Fables are simple stories which can be interpreted so that they teach a moral lesson, and these poems have clear messages even now, nearly twenty-six centuries later. La Fontaine expressed this view when he wrote of Aesop's fables: '*At first sight, I own, they are childish; but their childishness is the wrapping of weighty truths.*'

Look at the first part of the assignment:

- Explain the *literal meanings* and then the '*weighty truths*' of the three poems.

The literal meaning of a fable is what happens in the story, i.e. what it is primarily about. You could summarize the literal meaning of 'The Frog and the Ox' in this way:

The story in 'The Frog and the Ox' is about a frog who was envious of the huge size of an ox. She wanted to be as big as the ox, so she puffed herself up, but she puffed herself up so much that she burst.

Now write the same kind of brief summary of the stories in the other two poems, 'The Grasshopper and the Ant' and 'The Eagle and the Beetle'.

You have then explained the literal meanings of the three fables. Now you are ready for the 'weighty truths'.

What is this 'weighty truth'? It is the serious message or **moral** which lies 'underneath' the literal story. If you follow what La Fontaine said, you need to take off the childish '*wrapping*' to find it. In other words, we need to **interpret** the literal story. Perhaps a beetle or a frog represents a particular person, a type of person, or even a country. Perhaps the creature's behaviour is being criticized for being cruel or stupid.

Look at 'The Frog and the Ox'. Read it carefully and find the lines which express the moral of the fable. They are:

> '*In every rank* this form of nonsense rages:* (* level of society)
> *Each cit* must build a mansion like a lord,* (* citizen)
> *Each petty* prince must be ambassador'd*,* (* minor; * have ambassadors)
> *Each marquis* have his pages*.*' (* aristocrat; * royal attendants)

Obviously, the poet wants you to think these lines are important. He has set them out as a separate four-line **stanza**. The technical term for a four-line stanza, or verse, like this is a **quatrain**. This quatrain has a different **rhyme scheme** from the rest of the poem.

You need to explain first of all what the lines mean. Because this version of Aesop's fable was written by La Fontaine in 1668, some of the words are **archaic**, which means they are old and no longer used in modern writing. All the difficult words have been explained for you. The meaning of these final four lines can be explained in this way:

In the last four lines, the poet expresses the moral of the fable. He says that every ordinary citizen wants to build a big house for himself like a lord's, and every nobleman wants servants and other staff. In other words, people always want to be seen as having a higher status than they really do.

This explains the moral. Now you need to link the moral to the creatures in the poem:

The fate of the frog shows that no good will come to anyone who foolishly tries to appear more important than he or she really is. If people try very hard to be what they are not, like the frog, they will destroy themselves.

You have now explained both the literal meaning and the 'weighty truth' of 'The Frog and the Ox'. Now, following the above approach, write the same kind of explanation of the literal meanings and the 'weighty truths' of 'The Grasshopper and the Ant' and 'The Eagle and the Beetle'. You have now completed the first part of the assignment.

Now look at the second part of the assignment:

◆ Show how the words and verse structures give the creatures in the poems their own individual characters.

First of all we need to identify the creatures in the three fables. They are the frog, ox, grasshopper, ant, eagle, and beetle. Make a column for each of them. Then read the poems through, and write down some words that describe the characters of the creatures in the appropriate column as you read. You will be looking for words to describe them, like 'patient' or 'faithful'. You could start your eagle column this way:

Eagle
a) Proud
b) Uncaring

When you have completed your lists, you should have plenty of words describing character. You can **select** the ones you want to focus on. As an example, we'll start with the eagle.

Re-read the first three verses and find any words or phrases which suggest that the eagle is a proud and haughty bird. Amongst others, you will find these lines:

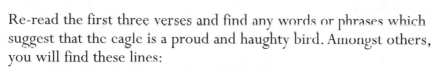

> 'But the great eagle sneered with pride'
>
> 'How do you dare assume the right
> To meddle with my appetite?'
>
> '... Have you not heard
> I am the great god Zeus's bird?'

To answer **how** the poet gives the creatures their characters, you need to **analyse** his choice of words and verse structure. Ask yourself these questions:

1. What does the word '*sneered*' in the phrase '*sneered with pride*' say to you?

EXAMINER'S TIP Most words in English beginning with a 'sn' sound are nasty in some way. Think of some examples, like snigger.

You could write:

We can tell that the eagle is a proud and haughty bird because when the beetle pleaded with her to spare her friend, she just 'sneered with pride'. 'Sneered' has a harsh sound and describes the superior, cruel way she ignored the beetle's cries.

2. How do the stress and associations of the word '*dare*' convey pride?

KEY TERM

'*Dare*' is a **monosyllable,** that is a word made up of one single syllable. It is easy to stress it: DARE. Stress **emphasizes** the word and, as the word '*dare*' conveys authority and anger, it emphasizes the eagle's authoritarian and cruel attitude.

You could explain it this way:

The eagle's cruel pride is also shown in her harsh reply to the beetle: 'How do you dare assume the right.' The stress falls on the monosyllable 'dare', which emphasizes the eagle's haughty and authoritarian attitude towards the beetle.

3. How does the verse structure help to make the eagle seem haughty?

First of all, you need to define the verse structure. The poem is written in **rhyming couplets**, that is where every two lines rhyme with each other. There are also a fixed number of syllables to each line. Count them and see how the poet keeps to this structure. How could you link this choice of verse structure to the eagle's character? You could write:

The poem is written in rhyming couplets and eight-syllable lines. This strict verse structure helps to make the eagle sound haughty and proud, because the control of the lines reinforces her controlling manner. She is inflexible, like the verse structure.

Select character qualities from your lists for each of the creatures and analyse the poet's choice of language and verse structure in the same way as above.

You have now completed the assignment.

The Frog and the Ox

by Jean de la Fontaine

translated by Edward March

A Frog beheld an Ox, with eyes
Of envy for his noble size;
So, being in all no bigger than an egg,
She needs must swell, and stretch, and strain,
    and puff,
To emulate the animal's proportions,
Saying 'Look, sister dear, I beg,
How am I getting on? Is that enough?'
'Not yet.' 'Then this?' 'Scarce better than at
    first.'
'Now?' 'Nothing like!' The end of her
    contortions
Was that the puny creature burst.

In every rank this form of nonsense rages:
    Each cit must build a mansion like a lord,
    Each petty prince must be ambassador'd,
    Each marquis have his pages.

The Grasshopper and the Ant

by Jean de la Fontaine

translated by Edward March

A Grasshopper the summer long
Sang her song,
And found herself when winter came
Without a morsel to her name.
Not one scrap of worm or fly
Had the careless thing put by!
So she took her tale of want
To her neighbour Mistress Ant,
Begging just a grain or two
Wherewithal to carry through
Till the Spring came round next year.
'I'll repay you, never fear,
Honest insect, 'ere the fall,
Interest and principal.'
One fault from which the Ant is free
Is making loans too readily.
'Tell me how you spent the summer.'
'Night and day, to every comer,
Please you, ma'am, I sang my ditty.'
'Singing, were you? Very pretty!
Now's your chance,
Mistress Grasshopper, to dance.'

The Eagle and the Beetle

by Vikram Seth

A beetle loved a certain hare
And wandered with him everywhere:
They went to fairs and feasts together,
Took walks in any kind of weather,
Talked of the future and the past
On sunny days or overcast,
But, since their friendship was so pleasant,
Lived for the most part in the present.

One day, alas, an eagle flew
Above them, and before they knew
What cloud had shadowed them, the hare
Hung from her talons in mid-air.
'Please spare my friend,' the beetle cried.
But the great eagle sneered with pride:
'You puny, servile, cloddish bug –
Go off and hide your ugly mug.
How do you dare assume the right
To meddle with my appetite?
This hare's my snack. Have you not heard
I am the great god Zeus's bird?
Nothing can harm me, least of all
A slow, pathetic, droning ball.
Here, keep your friend's head – ' And she tore
The hare's head off, and swiftly bore
His bleeding torso to her nest,
Ripped off his tail, and ate the rest.

The beetle stared at her friend's head,
And wished that she herself was dead.
She mixed her tears with his dark blood
And cloaked his face with clods of mud.
She swore that till her dying breath
She would avenge his cruel death,
That she would make the eagle pay
For what she had performed today.

Next day she slowly tracked the trail
From drop of blood to tuft of tail,
Till, high up on a mountain crest,
She found the huge unguarded nest,
And at the hour that yesterday
The bird had plunged towards her prey,
The beetle with her six short legs
Rolled out the mighty eagle's eggs.
She left at once, but she could hear
The eagle's screams of pain and fear
When later she returned and found
The broken eggshells on the ground.

Next day the eagle moved her nest
Ten miles or more towards the west,
But still the beetle's scrutiny
Followed her flight from rock to tree.
When finally the eagle laid
Another clutch, the beetle made
Straight for the nest in which they lay,
And, when the bird was hunting prey,
With much fatigue but little sound
Rolled the great eggs onto the ground.

When this had gone on for a year
The eagle, crazed with rage and fear,
Would turn back, screeching, in mid-air
Whenever she would sight a hare.
The far drone of the beetle's flight
Shattered her calm by day or night.
For weeks on end she scarcely slept.
She laid her eggs in grief, and wept
When what she'd feared had come to pass –
And her smashed brood lay on the grass.

At last she cried: 'What is the use
Of bearing your protection, Zeus –
When that small, evil clot of mud
Has massacred my flesh and blood?
King of the gods, where may I rest?
Where may I safely build my nest?
Where lay my eggs without mishap?'
'Here –' said the god. 'Here, in my lap.'

And so the eggs lay, more secure
Than they had ever lain before.
What in the universe could be
More safe than Zeus's custody?

So thought the eagle, till one day
The beetle saw them where they lay –
And, aiming with precision, flung
A microscopic ball of dung
Into the lap of mighty Zeus –
Who, rising, spewed divine abuse,
And, shaking dirt from off his legs,
Unthinkingly tipped out the eggs.
Past hope, the eagle pined away
And died of grief – and to this day
They say that eagles will not nest
In months when beetles fly their best;
But others, not so superstitious,
Merely assert that Fate's capricious,
And that the strong who crush the weak
May not be shown the other cheek.

POETRY UNIT 2

ASSIGNMENT

- Compare in one paragraph the theme of the two poems.
- Explain how the verse structure in 'just in case' is irregular. Why do you think the poet wrote the verses the way she did?
- How do the similes in 'On going from the province ...' deepen the meaning of the poem?

The texts for this assignment are on page 62.

CONTEXT

The Caribbean poet, Jean 'Binta' Breeze, wrote 'just in case' in 2000. She is a performance poet. Hitomaro was a Japanese poet who died at the beginning of the eighth century. This means that no less than thirteen hundred years separate these two poems, and half the globe separates the homelands of the two poets. However, an age-old theme unites them. That theme is love!

Look at the first part of the assignment:

- Compare in one paragraph the theme of the two poems.

Read the two poems twice, slowly. Enjoy the rhythm as you read.

You are asked to **compare** the theme in the two poems.

EXAMINER'S TIP

A **comparison** includes a consideration of features which are:
(a) similar **or** different, (b) similar **and** different.

It is clear here that the two poems share the theme of love, so you will be finding similarities in the theme. State this in your opening sentence. In the rest of your paragraph, expand on the similarity of the theme of love, by explaining:

a) the message the poet has for the one she loves in 'just in case'
b) how the poet feels about his separation from his wife in 'On going from the province ...'
c) the commitment of both poets to the ones they love
d) the use both poets make of nature to express their love

To demonstrate that you are comparing the theme in the poems and finding it similar, include **comparative phrases** such as: 'similarly', 'in the same way', 'like the first poem'.

When you have finished, look at the second part of the assignment:

◆ Explain how the verse structure of 'just in case' is irregular. Why do you think the poet wrote the verses the way she did?

K E Y
TERM

A **regular verse structure** is where there is a set number of lines to the verse or stanza. In addition, there might be a rhyme scheme and a set pattern of syllables and stresses to each line. An example of a regular verse structure can be seen in 'Once in a Lifetime, Snow' on page 69.

To explain how the verse structure here is **irregular**, you need to ask yourself certain questions. Write down the following questions and your answers to them:

1. How many lines does each verse have?
2. Is there a pattern to the number of syllables per line?
3. Is there a rhyme scheme?
4. How many capital letters are there in the poem and its title?
5. How much punctuation is used in the poem?
6. How many sentences are there in the complete poem?
7. How many times does the word 'and' appear?
8. What word does the poem open with?
9. Where would you usually find this word in a sentence?

Your answers should give you the data which will enable you to answer the first part of the question. You could start:

The five verses have between three and six lines each and there are between three and nine syllables in each line. This shows that the verse structure has no particular pattern and no rhyme scheme and is, therefore, irregular ...

Work through your findings in this way, showing the irregular verse structure of the poem.

You have covered **what** the poet did and now you have to analyse **why** she did it. In other words, you are being asked to analyse the **effects** of the poet's choices. For example, in your data above, you found that the poem starts with the word '*and*', written with a **lower case** 'a', not a capital 'A' as you would expect for the first word. You have found that 'and' is usually a **conjunction** which links a clause or phrase to the main clause of a sentence. It does not usually start a sentence. Now, you have to ask yourself: '**Why** did the poet write like this? What **effect** did she want to achieve?' You could write:

If I were talking to someone, I might well start a sentence 'and another thing' because it would follow on from what I was saying. It is used in speech and is, therefore, colloquial and informal. What the poet is saying to the man she loves is intimate, and the small 'a' suggests the poem is just part of an ongoing intimate conversation. To start in the middle of a conversation is a dramatic way to start because it immediately involves the reader.

Using this example as a guide, work through your other pieces of data and find reasons and effects for them. When you have done this, you will have completed this part of the assignment and will be ready for the last part:

◆ How do the similes in 'On going from the province . . . ' deepen the meaning of the poem?

First of all, you need to identify the similes. Go through the poem and write down the lines which feature comparisons introduced by the word '*like*' or '*as*'. You will find five. The first is:

'And deep as the deep-sea-weed, I long
For my love . . . '

When you have identified the five similes, you can begin to explain how they extend the meaning of the lines. First of all, explain the basic meaning of the lines. For the first simile you could write:

The poet is on the 'weed-locked' inland sea of Japan, sailing away from his wife. He misses her deeply. The longing which he feels for his wife is as deep as the sea-weed.

Next, add an explanation of how the simile **deepens the meaning**:

Comparing his longing for his wife with the 'deep-sea-weed' gives a vivid visual picture of the swirling weed in the depths of this Japanese sea. It also conveys the depth of his longing.

Now go back to the other four similes and work through them in the same way. Be concise in your explanations. When you have done this, you will have finished this assignment.

just in case

by Jean 'Binta' Breeze

and just in case
you ever wonder
if I am the passing summer's sun

and if a winter night of doubt
should wake you
and you think I am the snow
that's suddenly gone

and if on lonely mornings
you look up at the sky
and think I am a drifting cloud
that drops its rain
and mistlike
disappears

and if you ever think
some passing storm of frenzy
could wipe out all the pages
of our days

just give me time, my love
to come again
and touch you
with forever

On going from the province of Iwami, leaving his wife behind

by Hitomaro
translated from the original Japanese

Off the cape of Kara
In the weed-locked sea of Iwami,
The sea-pines needle the stones,
The sea-kelp litters the shallows.

And deep as the deep-sea-weed, I long
For my love who leaned sleeping against me,
As the sea-weed leans on the wave:
(alas, there were not many such nights)
Yet, I have come, left her behind,
Untwined her, like ivy, from me
And now that I bend back with longing,
As the sea-weed bends on the wave,
I cannot see the red sleeves of my love
Through the red-leaved falling confusion
On the oaks of mountain Watari.
Her sleeves have dissolved and gone
As the moon goes under the scud
Of the clouds on mountain Yakami.
The haze is risen. The evening is woven.
Lo, though I thought myself a man.
The thin stuff of my sleeves is wet with tears.

POETRY UNIT 3

ASSIGNMENT

♦ Compare the responses to snow and wet in the two poems.
♦ Explain how the rhythm and rhyme contribute to the gentle
  atmosphere of 'Once in a Lifetime, Snow'.
♦ Explore the humour in 'Such is Holland!'

The texts
for this
assignment
are on
page 69.

CONTEXT

In 'Once in a Lifetime, Snow' the Australian poet describes how his
uncle, a farmer, reacts to a rare, once-in-a-lifetime fall of snow in
Australia in the 1990s. In 'Such is Holland!' the Dutch poet in the
1890s complains about the constant wet and damp of his country's
climate.

Look at the first part of the assignment:

♦ Compare the responses to snow and wet in the two poems.

You are asked to **compare** the responses of the Australian farmer to
the snow and the Dutch poet to the wet. This means you make a
comparison in which you explain how the responses are similar *or*
different, or both similar *and* different, as appropriate.

So, to start with, you need to establish what the responses are. Start
with 'Once in a Lifetime, Snow'. Read it twice, carefully. Now go
through it, and write down the lines from which you can **interpret**
the farmer's reaction to the rare snowfall. Leave a couple of lines blank
underneath each of your quotations. Your list will start:

a) 'And he stopped short, and gazed'
b) 'And half his wrinkles vanished
   murmuring Snow.'
c) 'he stared to see
   the facts of weather raised
   to a mystery'

When you've finished, you'll have quite a long list. End your list with
the final four lines of the poem. Now go back to your blank lines.
Write down words and phrases which sum up the farmer's response,
which you have interpreted from the quotation.

For example, you might write:

a) surprise, disbelief
b) his face was blank with amazement
c) awe at the mysterious strangeness of the snow

Work through your list of quotations like this until you come to the final one. To understand the farmer's response completely, you need to explore the metaphorical meaning of these final four lines, when the farmer goes back into the house to waken '*a murmuring child*':

> '*Then, turning, he tiptoed in*
> *to a bedroom, smiled,*
> *and wakened a murmuring child*
> *and another child.*'

You will assume that the '*murmuring child*' in the bedroom is his sleeping son with whom he is going to share the excitement of the snow. His son is **literally** a child. But there is '*another child*' whom the farmer has wakened. This is a **metaphorical** child. Who / what / where is this other 'child'? Write your explanation.

You can now complete your written answer to this part of the assignment and then turn to the other poem 'Such is Holland!'

Read the poem twice carefully. Write out the lines where the poet mentions himself and his response to the wetness of his country, and leave a couple of lines blank underneath each one. You will find there are only three quotations:

a) 'Hear the autumnal plaint of a poet with a cold.'

b) '... No song, no joy, no peace for me.'

c) '... O land our forbears plotted
And, not at my request, extorted from the sea.'

In your blank lines, write phrases which sum up the poet's response to the wet.
Under the first quotation you could write:

sick and tired of the wet autumns – complaining that he has a miserable cold

Next, fill in your blank lines under the other two quotations. Now you are ready to write up in full the poet's response. Remember that you are **comparing** this poet's response with the Australian farmer's response to the snow in the other poem. So, write an introductory topic sentence which makes a comparison between the two. Because you have found differences rather than similarities between the responses, your introductory sentence could be:

The farmer marvels at the rare fall of snow in Australia, whereas the Dutch poet is sick of the constant wet and damp of his country.

To demonstrate that you are **comparing** the two sets of responses, include **comparative phrases**, such as: 'On the other hand ...', 'In contrast ...', 'Unlike the farmer ...', 'A different response ...'

When you have completed the comparison, you have finished the first part of the assignment and are ready for the second part:

◆ Explain how the rhythm and rhyme contribute to the gentle atmosphere of 'Once in a Lifetime, Snow'.

Sometimes you know that a poem *is* a poem just because it has broken up lines: it has no rhyme scheme, no verse structure, and no rhythm. With this poem, it is different. Ask yourself:

1. Is there a pattern to the **rhythm**, i.e. is there a set number of syllables that are stressed and unstressed?
2. Is there a pattern to the number of **syllables** to the line?
3. Is there a **rhyme scheme**?

Your answer to these questions should be 'Yes!' Now write down the details of these rhythm and rhyme patterns:

Rhythm: *the stress pattern for each verse is three stresses in lines 1 and 3; two stresses in lines 2 and 4, with one or two unstressed syllables between stresses*
Syllable count: *for most verses - 6 4 6 4. Sometimes lines 'borrow' syllables from their neighbours.*
Rhyme scheme: *for each verse - a b c b (i.e. lines 2 and 4 rhyme; lines 1 and 3 do not rhyme).*

Finding out the answers to these questions is a matter of looking carefully, counting, and finding patterns. The next step is to ask:

How do the poet's choices of rhyme scheme and rhythm contribute to the atmosphere of gentleness in the poem?

To start with, look at the **rhyme scheme** more closely. Make a list of all the words which rhyme with each other:

'raw' 'more'
'dawn' 'gone' (remember this is Australian!)
'ground' 'around'
'below' 'snow'
etc.

What do these words have in common? They all have **long vowels** or **diphthongs**.

Short vowels are heard in cat, pet, cot
Long vowels are heard in cart, peat, coot
A **diphthong** is two vowels together which make one long vowel sound: the 'i' sound in 'smiled' is made up of the two vowel sounds 'a' + 'ee'; the 'ou' sound in 'around' is made up of 'a' + 'oo'

Now, consider **how** these vowels contribute to the atmosphere of gentleness. Make a list of ten words such as 'whack' or 'quick!' which sound dramatic or harsh. Think of lullabies and make a list of another ten words which sound soothing and gentle. Now compare the vowels in the words in your list. You should find that long vowels often have a soothing effect.

You can now use your work on this section to explain the rhyme scheme in detail *and* how the long vowels and diphthongs help to create the gentle atmosphere of the poem.

Next, look at the stress pattern more closely. You have already noted that the number of stresses to the line is in the pattern of 3 2 3 2. On which word does the final stress fall in each line? You should find that the final stress falls on the last word in each line.

You may notice something else about the final stress on the final word. Although these words are at the end of the line, often they are not the end of a sentence. This means that the sense of the line carries on to the next line, for example:

> 'he stooped to break the sheer
> crust with delight
> at finding the cold unknown
> so deeply bright,'

KEY TERM

A line that ends with a full stop is called **end-stopped**. When consecutive lines are not end-stopped and the sense is carried on, it is called **enjambment**. The enjambment throughout this poem allows the lines to flow smoothly into one another.

Write a paragraph explaining the details of the rhythm. Then write another paragraph in which you use all the findings above to explain **how** the stresses in the rhythm help to create the gentle atmosphere of the poem. Finally, explain how the enjambment also contributes to this gentle atmosphere.

Now you are ready for the final part of the assignment:

◆ Explain the humour in 'Such is Holland!'

A humorous poem, film or play can make you fall off your chair laughing, or it might just make you smile. It's a spontaneous reaction, but when you explain **how** or **why** it makes you laugh or smile, you have to think. In your consideration of the humour in this poem, focus on these three headings:

The exclamation mark in the title

What is the tone of a poem called 'Such is Holland' (without an exclamation mark) likely to be? Do you think the tone of a poem called 'Such is Holland!' (with an exclamation mark) would be any different? Explain the function of the exclamation mark in this poem's title and relate it to the humorous tone of the poem. You need to ask yourself: 'Is the poet being serious? Is he being ironic?'

Exaggeration

Exaggeration is frequently a source of humour in films and jokes. '*O, land of unplumbed bogs, of roads resembling rivers*' is an example of exaggeration in this poem. Notice how the poet uses lists. You could relate the exaggeration and the use of lists to the humour in this way:

This line is part of the poet's long list of wet, damp characteristics of his country. The lists are humorous because they bring together many different things that are all unpleasant or ridiculous. This list is an exaggeration and so is the phrase 'roads resembling rivers'. The alliteration makes it humorous in its sound and the image of untamed water which it creates is absurd. The 'unplumbed bogs' is also an exaggeration as it suggests that the Dutch bogs are so deep that they cannot be measured. The absurdity is a source of humour.

Find another example of exaggeration and explain the humour in it, following the above as an example.

The use of the address 'O' throughout the poem

Where have you heard the word 'O' used to address someone? Christian prayers and hymns often address God as 'O Lord' or 'O God'. Classical poets would often address the Muses in this way, asking for inspiration. Shakespeare uses it in his plays, as does Milton in 'Paradise Lost'.

It is a rhetorical and serious form of address associated with a lofty subject, like a prayer to God or a request for inspiration in a great work. How is it used here?

'*O, spongy porridge-swamp, O homeland of galoshes*'

Instead of 'O' being followed by some elevated prayer or desire, it is followed by a comical description of the country as a mass of bog as wet as porridge. This contrast between lofty expectations and the triviality of what actually follows is called **bathos** and the effect is **bathetic**. It is a form of humour and a technique used in comedy sketches. (Perhaps you can think of an example?) Find two other examples of this use of the address 'O' in the poem and explain the humour in them using the above explanation as a guide.

You have now completed the assignment.

Once in a Lifetime, Snow
by Les Murray

Winters at home brought wind,
black frost and raw
grey rain in barbed-wire fields,
but never more

until the day my uncle
rose at dawn
and stepped outside — to find
his paddocks gone,

his cattle to their hocks
in ghostly ground
and unaccustomed light
for miles around.

And he stopped short, and gazed
lit from below,
and half his wrinkles vanished
murmuring Snow.

A man of farm and fact
he stared to see
the facts of weather raised
to a mystery

white on the world he knew
and all he owned.
Snow? Here? he mused. I see.
High time I learned.

Here, guessing what he meant
had much to do
with that black earth dread old men
are given to,

he stooped to break the sheer
crust with delight
at finding the cold unknown
so deeply bright,

at feeling it take his prints
so softly deep,
as if it thought he knew
enough to sleep,

or else, so little he
might seek to shift
its weight of wintry light
by a single drift,

perceiving this much, he scuffed
his slippered feet
and scooped a handful up
to taste, and eat

in memory of the fact
that even he
might not have seen the end
of reality …

Then, turning, he tiptoed in
to a bedroom, smiled,
and wakened a murmuring child
and another child.

Such is Holland!
by Petrus Augustus de Genestet
translated by Adriaan Barnouw

O, land of mud and mist, where man is wet and shivers
    Soaked with humidity, with damp and chilly dew,
    O, land of unplumbed bogs, of roads resembling rivers,
Land of umbrellas, gout, colds, agues, toothache, flu,

O, spongy porridge-swamp, O homeland of galoshes,
    Of cobblers, toads and frogs, peat diggers, mildew, mould,
    Of ducks and every bird that slobbers, splutters, splashes,
Hear the autumnal plaint of a poet with a cold.

Thanks to your clammy clime my arteries are clotted
    With blood turned mud. No song, no joy, no peace for me.
    You're fit for clogs alone, O land our forebears plotted
And, not at my request, extorted from the sea.

POETRY UNIT 4

ASSIGNMENT

- ◆ Explore the similarity of theme between the two poems.
- ◆ How do the two poets use language to convey mood?

The texts for this assignment are on page 74.

CONTEXT

In 'Mal du Pays' the Romanian people, driven by their yearning for the country from which they have been exiled, keep close to their only link to it: the station, the trains and the rail tracks. In 'A Blind Man Sings to His City' a blind man walks around his war-damaged Bosnian city and, although he cannot see, his senses give him an understanding of it which those who *can* see do not possess.

Look at the first part of the assignment:

- ◆ Explore the similarity of theme between the two poems.

KEY TERM

What is meant by **theme**? If we think of an **abstract noun** that sums up the **subject** or **topic** of the poem, we have identified a theme. An abstract noun is the name for a quality or concept which we cannot touch. For example, one theme of Wordsworth's poem, 'The Prelude' is *childhood*.

Read the two poems and then think of abstract nouns which convey the themes. A start has been made for you. The first word for 'Mal du Pays' is a translation of the poem's French title:

'Mal du Pays'
a) homesickness
b) exile

'A Blind Man Sings to His City'
a) blindness
b) love

Having suggested words for the themes, you will now be feeling more familiar with the poems, and will be able to decide on a theme which is common to both poems. As an example, take the theme of **loss**.

Write a topic sentence which explains concisely the theme of loss in each poem. You could start like this:

The people in both poems have lost something precious - in 'Mal du Pays' the Romanians have lost their homes through exile, and in 'A Blind Man Sings to His City' the man has lost his sight.

You will need to write a few more sentences explaining the loss in more **detail**. Look through the poems and write down brief **quotations** which you can use to support your explanation.

When you have written those sentences, explore the theme further. Imagine how you yourself might feel about such a loss. How would you react? Would you complain loudly? Lose all hope and sink into depression? Turn to religion for support? Try to make the best of it?

How do the people in the poems react to their loss? Write another sentence or two, this time summarizing how the people in the poems are similar in their reactions to their loss. Here is an example:

The blind man and the Romanians are not in despair as might be expected. The blind man actually 'sings' to his city and the Romanians seem comforted by the railway station, which they feel is a link with home.

To flesh out this summary, you need to explain the blind man's 'singing', and the comfort which the Romanians find in their situation. **Select** appropriate detail and brief quotation for your explanation. Write a paragraph for each poem. You could continue like this:

In 'Mal du Pays' the exiled Romanians find comfort in feeling 'closer to their country', to which they are connected by the railway lines: 'They're in permanent communication/with home.'

You could begin your paragraph on the second poem this way:

In 'A Blind Man Sings to His City' the speaker has lost his sight, but he has the compensation of being able to 'see only what others don't' through the physical sensations he experiences. He even feels that his blindness is a blessing given by God.

You have now explored the similarity of the theme of loss in the two poems. For further practice, choose another theme and explain and illustrate its similarity in the two poems in the same way.

Now look at the second part of the assignment:

◆ How do the two poets use language to convey mood?

Mood is another name for the atmosphere in a poem. The mood could be, for example, optimistic, melancholy, sombre, light-hearted or triumphant. Different poems have different moods and mood can change within a poem. It is the poet's use of language which enables us to feel the **mood**.

What is the **mood** in 'Mal du Pays'? Ask yourself about the people's thoughts and feelings. If you think they feel sad, you could explore the **mood of sadness**. If you think they are homesick you could explore the **mood of longing**. We will consider how the mood of longing is conveyed through the poet's use of language.

> *'They want to be closer to their country.'*
>
> *'This gives them the feeling*
> *they're not too far away.'*

These quotations are simple statements of fact, telling us of the Romanians' desire to feel closer to home. To explore the poet's use of language in these lines, you could make a checklist like this:

Vocabulary - simple
Word length - mostly monosyllables (words of one syllable)
Metaphorical language - there isn't any
Modifiers (adjectives, adverbs) - no significant ones
Sentence structure – simple, like conventional prose
Rhythm - like ordinary prose
Rhyme scheme - the lines don't rhyme

How can you link these findings to what you are being asked: to explain how the poet's use of words conveys the mood of longing? You could start this way:

The simple statements clearly convey the desires of the exiled people to feel closer to home. The simplicity of the words, the lack of modifiers and metaphorical language make the longing understated. This controlled, unpoetic language is effective because it emphasizes the quiet, uncomplaining behaviour of the people as they long for their home.

Now, look at another quotation:

> 'Romanians sit sadly on their luggage
> and listen to their homesick yearnings
> in untranslatable seismic quivers
> shuddering down a steel rail.'

Fill in your checklist again:

Vocabulary - complex: 'seismic'; 'untranslatable'
    emotive: 'yearnings'
Word length - mostly two syllables; polysyllabic (many
    syllables): 'untranslatable'
Metaphorical language - the yearnings expressed through
    vibration of the railway lines
Modifiers - most nouns are modified: adverb 'sadly'
Sentence structure - like prose, complex
Rhythm - like prose
Rhyme scheme - the lines don't rhyme

Your observations are different this time. How can you link these to the poet's use of language in conveying the mood of longing? You could start this way:

The mood of longing in the previous two quotations was
understated. Now in the final four lines of the poem, it is expressed
more forcefully. To begin with, the Romanians are presented as a
group sitting 'sadly on their luggage', just sitting quietly
longing, but then the language becomes more powerful. 'Their
homesick yearnings' is a strongly emotive phrase. Their longing
is no longer subdued, but has become 'untranslatable seismic
quivers'. With its associations with earthquakes, 'seismic'
suggests the passion of their longings, and 'shuddering' suggests
both emotion and violence. This is the climax of the poem, where
the enormous strength and depth of the exiles' longing is conveyed.

Now, turn to 'A Blind Man Sings to His City' and select a mood which you feel is conveyed in the poem. You might select sadness or something else. Analyse the poet's language as you did for 'Mal du Pays'. When you have done this, you will have completed the assignment.

Mal du Pays

by Marin Sorescu
translated John H Williams and Hilde Ollschofski

When Romanians
exile themselves,
they sit down by the railway tracks
of Europe.
Or at the station, if it's not too crowded.

They want to be closer to their country.
Able to catch the first train there,
at any time.

This gives them the feeling
they're not too far away.
They walk along the tracks.
They listen to the whistle of trains.
They're in permanent communication
with home.

In spring, especially,
when earth's magnetism
unsettles the cranes in flight,
Romanians sit sadly on their luggage
and listen to their homesick yearnings
in untranslatable seismic quivers
shuddering down a steel rail.

A Blind Man Sings to His City

by Abdulah Sidran
translated by Ted Hughes & Antonela Glavinic

The rain stops. Now from the drains,
From the attics, from under the floorboards
Of the shattered homes in the suburbs
Oozes the stench of the corpses
Of mice. I walk seeking
No special meaning in this. A blind man,
To whom it has been given to see
Only what others don't. This
Makes up for my deprivation: in the south
        wind
That touches me I recognise the voices
Of those who left this city. As if they were
        crying.
There, scent of the linden trees, close.
I know
The bridge is near, where my step and my
        stick
Will ring differently – more light
In the sound. There, now, right by my ear
Two flies mate in the air.
It will be scorching hot again. Bodies
Brush past me, hot,
Smelling of bed, smelling of lust. I walk
        muttering
To God, as if He were beside me:
'Surely nobody knows this city
Better than me – better than me, God,
To whom you have given never to see
The face he loves.'

WRITING INTRODUCTION

In the examination, you have two writing tasks:

1. Paper 1 Section B sets you a task on the three writing skills: ARGUE, PERSUADE, ADVISE.
2. Paper 2 Section B sets you a task on the three writing skills: ANALYSE, REVIEW, COMMENT.

Each question could focus on **one** or **two** or all **three** of the elements in the triplet.

THE STRUCTURE OF THIS SECTION

In the following section, there are six writing units: one each on Argue, Persuade, Advise, Analyse, Review, and Comment. This is to give you experience and understanding of each one. However, as you work through them, you will notice that the elements in each triplet overlap. If you are **arguing** against air travel being the greatest invention of the last one hundred years, for example, you will be trying to **persuade** your audience at the same time; or if you **review** a period of your life, you will be **analysing** the significance of events.

In this section, you will find:

*   **examples** of the sorts of writing tasks you could be asked to complete in the examination: a letter, a report, a written speech, an advice column reply, and a magazine article;
*   specimen students' answers with examiner's comments;
*   the **conventions** (rules) you must follow for each kind of writing, e.g. how to lay out a formal letter;
*   guidance on **register** (that is, the tone of your writing), which needs to be appropriate to your **audience**. For example, readers of your school magazine might appreciate a little humour, whereas if you are asked to write a report to your head teacher on a proposed change to school rules, humorous comments would be inappropriate;
*   tasks for you to complete yourself, using the guidance that you've been given.

ORGANIZING YOUR WRITING

Organizing ideas into paragraphs

You will find guidance on:
- how to spend some time before you start writing on organizing your ideas into topics and paragraphs;
- how to use paragraphs to mark the development or stages in your writing.

Remember:

- to indent your paragraphs clearly;
- to leave a line between paragraphs if your handwriting is the sort that gets tangled up in the line below.

Sentence construction and punctuation

- If you leave **full stops** out, or use commas instead, the reader will not be able to make sense of what you write. Think of a comma as marking a brief pause and a full stop as marking the place where the reader will pause and take a breath. Allow enough time to read through your writing, and check your full stops.
- Use simple sentences **and** complex sentences with connectives, e.g. 'but', 'whereas', 'similarly', 'next'.
- Don't use double (or triple!!!) exclamation marks.
- Remember how **quotation** and **speech marks** are used to show:
  1. direct speech, e.g. "I won't!" she shrieked.
  2. the name of a film or book, e.g. We are reading 'Jane Eyre'.
  3. a quotation or a saying, e.g. 'Laugh and the world laughs with you' as they say.

The points below are all illustrated in the following units.
- Adventurous and varied sentence structure chosen for effect, e.g. verbless sentences, commands, rhetorically balanced sentences and questions, exclamations, quotations, direct speech.
- Varied punctuation used for effect, e.g. dashes, parenthetical brackets and commas; semi-colons; exclamation marks; quotation marks.

Vocabulary

Words are the only tools you have to reach your audience and express the lively ideas and feelings you have in your head.

◆ Check for dull, limited words like '*good*', '*bad*' or '*nice*' in your writing, and for any repetition of words or phrases. Cross them out and write more demanding, vivid words over the top.

humiliating

'It was a ~~bad~~ experience'.

an idyllic

'My grandmother had ~~a nice~~ garden'.

◆ Don't use clichés, e.g. '*over the moon*' and '*over the top*'.
◆ Don't use colloquialisms or slang expressions.
◆ Do use vivid and interesting words.

Spelling

Make sure that you can spell:
◆ everyday words in common use such as '*can't*' and '*father*';
◆ confusing word pairs such as '*were*' and '*we're*', '*your*' and '*you're*';
◆ words given to you in the question.

Remember it is always better to use (and spell wrongly) an adventurous word like, for example, '*inspirational*' to describe your teacher, rather than to use a dull word you can spell like '*good*'.

Learn how apostrophes are used to show:
◆ when a letter or letters have been left out (omission), e.g. '*it's*', '*I'll*', '*we've*';
◆ when something belongs to someone or something (possession) '*Matthew's*', '*children's*'.

Handwriting

If you write illegibly in your examination, you will lose marks. Check your handwriting! It really is worth learning how to write correctly. Remember that neat, legible handwriting always makes a very favourable impression.

◆ If the key word in a subtle point you're making is illegible, you will not be credited for it.
◆ Dot your i's, don't put circles over them.
◆ If you form your capital letters in the same way as your lower case letters, it will look as though you don't know that a sentence starts with a capital letter.

WRITING UNIT 1: ARGUE

INTRODUCTION

One type of writing you need to practise is presenting an argument. In the examination, you may be asked to write this in the form of a speech. Look at the example below and the explanation that follows.

> ### STUDENTS' TASK
> Your year group is holding a debate. The motion is 'Mobile phones are the best invention of the last fifty years'. Write out your speech in full, arguing either for or against the motion.

Here is one student's complete written speech in response:

Madam chairman, ladies and gentlemen, lend me your ears – that is if they don't already have a mobile phone stuck to them! Own up, how many of you have a mobile? I thought so, just about everyone in this room. They're obviously a must-have possession, but are they the best invention in the last fifty years?

It all depends on what you mean by 'best'. Best at annoying people? Yes! How many of you have been brought to the brink of violence on the bus as the person beside you bleats banal details of their night out into their latest top-of-the-range mobile? Best at introducing yet more peer group pressure? Yes, again. In some circles, unless you've got a phone that vibrates when you tell it to, plays Westlife's latest single in a series of annoying beeps, and tells you the time in Hong Kong, then you're an outcast. Even better at inciting a new crime boom? Absolutely! Thousands of mobile phones are stolen every day in Britain and many of these thefts involve violence.

However, no one here could deny that mobile phones are ingenious inventions. They have revolutionized the way we communicate. They have been used to summon help in emergencies and have arguably saved lives; our parents give us more freedom because they can use them to track us. The records of calls made provide police with valuable clues in criminal investigations; they enabled husbands and wives to say their terrible goodbyes on September 11th; they have provided millions of people worldwide with employment in their production. But does this make them the best invention of the last fifty years?

I would argue, ladies and gentlemen, that it definitely does not. Yes, an emergency call from a mobile phone can save a life, but the number of lives saved that way is completely insignificant in comparison with those lives saved by dialysis machines, by advances in cancer treatment, and by organ transplants. To suggest otherwise is ludicrous. For every life saved by a mobile phone, hundreds are blighted by the avarice they create; whereas if someone receives a new kidney, all of their family receives a new life as well. How can these crime-inducing fashion accessories, requiring monstrous steel aerials which clutter our skylines, possibly be called the best invention of the last fifty years, when compared with the life-giving advances in medicine? A mobile phone gives us a social life. A pacemaker gives us a life.

WRITING THE TEXT OF A SPEECH

1. Write a punchy introductory sentence which will immediately grab the attention of the audience: ask a direct question; be witty or outrageous (but not *too* outrageous!).
2. Involve your audience throughout: ask direct questions which require yes/no answers or a show of hands; ask rhetorical questions (which raise issues but do not require direct answers); use the second-person pronoun *'you'*.
3. Provoke a response from your audience: be emphatic; be opinionated; exaggerate a little for effect; appeal to their emotions.
4. Choose vocabulary which will amuse, surprise, provoke, move, impress your audience – be inventive and ambitious!
5. Use a variety of sentence structures to keep your audience engaged and involved, and to convince them.

THE ORGANIZATION OF A SPEECH

1. Open your argument with a direct address to your audience, e.g. *'Madam [or Mr] chairman, ladies and gentlemen'*.
2. Conclude your writing effectively. This can be done in different ways:
    ◆ formally, e.g. *'Ladies and gentlemen, I rest my case.'*
    ◆ less formally, e.g. *'Thank you for listening.'*
    ◆ with an effective final point which sums up your argument, e.g. *'A mobile phone gives us a social life. A pacemaker gives us a life.'*
3. Plan your paragraphs. Make notes so that each paragraph marks a stage in your argument.

EXAMINER'S COMMENTS

Here are an Examiner's comments on the example student's speech. You can use them as a checklist when you write your response to the task at the end of this unit.

Communication

✓ A range of persuasive and dynamic ideas is clearly communicated.
✓ Awareness and involvement of the audience is shown in appropriate address (*'ladies and gentlemen'*); personal pronoun *'you'*; reference to place (*'everyone in this room'*).
✓ The register for a speech is appropriate.
✓ An extended vocabulary is shown in the range of chosen language: appropriately colloquial (*'a must-have possession'*); emotive (*'their terrible goodbyes'*); sophisticated (*'blighted by the avarice they create'*); hyphenated adjectives used for effect (*'crime-inducing'*).

✓ Rhetorical questions are used effectively to involve the audience and to mark the development of the argument (*'But does this make them the best invention of the last fifty years?'*).

✓ The first sentence is humorous, witty, sophisticated, and arresting.

✓ Connectives and phrases are chosen especially in order to argue effectively, e.g. starting a sentence with a connective (*'But does this make ...?'*), or with a phrase that develops the argument (*'I would argue, ladies and gentlemen, ...'*; *'Yes,...,but...'*).

✓ Sophisticated language is chosen for effect, e.g. alliteration in *'bleats banal details'* chosen to express disapproval.

✓ There is well-controlled irony in the choice of examples.

✓ An emphatic conclusion is effectively made.

Organization of ideas

✓ Paragraphs are clearly planned to enhance the development and effectiveness of the argument.

✓ The introductory paragraph is effectively brief and punchy.

✓ The ideas are fully developed, coherent and raise complex issues.

✓ Issues are compared and contrasted (e.g. benefits/limitations; saving lives by mobiles/medicine.

Range and accuracy

✓ The sentence demarcation is accurate.

✓ A wide variety of punctuation is used successfully for effect: exclamation marks for humour (*'mobile phone stuck to them!'*) and emphasis (*'Absolutely!'*); semi-colons linking main clauses to give weight to the evidence provided; question marks for a variety of question types; commas denoting phrases or words in parenthesis (*'I would argue, ladies and gentlemen,'*); a dash to convey a pause.

✓ A wide variety of sentence structures is used successfully for effect: brief verbless sentences used for emphasis, to mark stages in the development of the argument, and to involve the audience (*'Yes, again'*; *'Absolutely'*); brief sentences used for emphasis and dramatic effect (*'To suggest otherwise is ludicrous.'*).

✓ There is accurate spelling of ambitious words, e.g. *'blighted'*, *'inciting'*, *'ludicrous'*.

YOUR TASK

Now write your response to the following task. Your year group is holding a debate. Write out a speech in full, arguing either for or against the motion: 'Air travel is the greatest invention of the last one hundred years.'

WRITING UNIT 2: PERSUADE

INTRODUCTION

Persuasive writing aims to persuade someone to do something or to agree with a point of view. In your examination you may be asked to write a persuasive letter. Look at the example below and the explanation that follows.

> ## STUDENTS' TASK
> Charles Skinner is an expedition leader. He is organizing a trip for a group of young people to a wildlife centre in central Africa, to see gorillas in the wild. He has advertised in Go travel magazine for young people to apply for one *free* place on the trip. Write a letter to him to persuade him to choose *you* for the free place.

Here is one student's response to this task:

The Expedition Leader   4 Westwood Crescent
'Go'   Bath BA4 8ET
Sheffield S4 6DY   10 June 2002

Dear Mr Skinner

    I have seen your advertisement in 'Go' travel magazine asking for young people to tell you why they would like to join your gorilla watch trip to central Africa. I am writing to tell you why I would <u>love</u> to join your group.

    I have been very interested in wildlife all my life but my one huge love is gorillas. I have posters of them in my room and have studied books and films about them. I have watched them in the zoo on many occasions, but that has always been through the bars of a cage. When I saw your advertisement, I just couldn't believe it. I have always dreamed of seeing wild gorillas in their own habitat for as long as I can remember and here was a chance of my wildest dream coming true!

    I've never had the chance to work with gorillas, but I have belonged to our local Pony Rescue Association since I was thirteen. On Saturdays I help with the rescued ponies. Last year I took part in a sponsored run to raise money for the Association and collected £250. I am used to working with others in school sports teams and at the stables. I get on well with people my own age and with adults and I'm very reliable. I am planning to be a veterinary nurse when I leave school.

    I've never been abroad because we are a big family and we can't afford holidays. This trip would be the most fantastic experience of my whole life. You are the only person in the world who can make my dream come true.

Yours sincerely

Sarah Manners

Miss Sarah Manners

REGISTER

The purpose of a **formal persuasive letter** is to persuade somebody the writer doesn't know. The **tone** or **register** must be appropriate to the task, and the **language** must be formal. This means the writer must be polite and respectful and use the kind of language he or she would use in a job interview. Slang is obviously out. Excessive pleading, such as *'Please, please, PLEASE choose me!'*, or threatening language, are inappropriate in a persuasive letter. Think of some persuasive phrases, such as: *'Please would you consider'*; *'Please would you help'*; *'How exciting it would be'*; *'This is a unique opportunity for me'*.

THE LAYOUT OF A FORMAL LETTER

Include the following in the layout of a formal letter:
1. your address in the top right-hand corner (don't include your name);
2. the date, including the year, e.g. 10/6/02 or 10 June 2002;
3. the title of the addressee (the person to whom you are writing) on the left-hand side, e.g. *'The Expedition Leader'*;
4. the address of the addressee underneath his or her name;
5. an appropriate salutation (opening), e.g. *'Dear Mr Skinner'* or *'Dear Sir'*;
6. an appropriate signing off, e.g. *'Yours sincerely'* if you started with *'Dear Mr Skinner'* or *'Yours faithfully'* if you started with *'Dear Sir'*;
7. your signature;
8. your name printed underneath, e.g. *'Miss Sarah Manners'*;
9. correct punctuation (either none at all in the layout of the addresses and dates, as in word processing, OR with commas and full stops).

PLANNING AND ORGANIZING A FORMAL LETTER

Plan before you start writing the body of the letter, e.g. what sort of reasons would you use to try to persuade the expedition leader to choose you? What interests, character qualities, and experience would he want to see in you? In this case, he would definitely want to see:

◆ an enormous enthusiasm
◆ a sincere interest in gorillas
◆ appropriate career plans
◆ an ability to get on with other people

Make a brief plan of what you are going to write in each of your paragraphs. Remember that if you're writing this kind of letter in an examination, it doesn't have to be true!

EXAMINER'S COMMENTS

Here are an Examiner's comments on the example student's letter. You can use them as a checklist when you write your own response to the task at the end of this unit.

Communication

✓ The meaning is clear in every sentence.
✓ The purpose and audience are clear throughout.
✓ The register for persuasion is appropriate, with the writer conveying her enthusiasm and her suitable character.
✓ The language is chosen specifically to persuade ('*You are the only person in the world who can*'; '*my one huge love is gorillas*').
✓ Some detail is selected to emphasize the deserving nature of her family situation ('*we are a big family and we can't afford holidays*').
✓ The vocabulary is appropriate, if unadventurous: 'passion' would be a more developed word than '*huge love*'; '*dream come true*' is repeated.

Organization of ideas

✓ The paragraphs are clearly organized.
✓ The paragraphs are of varying lengths for different purposes, e.g. short introductory and final paragraphs.
✓ The evidence used to persuade Charles Skinner is coherent, organized, and reasonably developed.

Range and accuracy

✓ The letter layout is accurate.
✓ There is some varied sentence structure: one final brief persuasive sentence; complex sentences for conveying information.
✓ The sentence division is accurate, i.e. full stops in the right places.
✓ The spelling is accurate, including '*sponsored*' and '*veterinary*'.
✓ An exclamation mark is used to convey enthusiasm and excitement.
✓ The clauses are correctly demarcated with commas ('*When I saw your advertisement, I*').
✓ Basic connectives are correctly used in complex sentences, e.g. '*because*', '*but*', '*and*'.

YOUR TASK

Now write your response to the following task. A youth leader is running an outdoors activity week in the Lake District, where there will be a wide choice of activities, including rock climbing, abseiling, and horse riding. He has advertised for young people to apply for one *free* place on the trip. Write a letter to the youth leader to try to persuade him to choose *you* for the free place.

WRITING UNIT 3: ADVISE

INTRODUCTION

Sometimes in the examination you will be asked to write a text which advises the reader about something. Look at the example below, which is in the form of a magazine problem page. Then read the explanation that follows.

> ### STUDENTS' TASK
> You are an advice column writer for the problem page of a magazine, and have received the following letter:
>
> 'I am thirteen years old and very miserable. I'm bullied every day by two pupils who are older than I am and now I'm scared to go to school. What should I do?'
>
> Write a reply to this letter for your problem page, in which you advise the writer of the letter what to do.

Here is one student's complete answer:

We're Here to Help – Your Problems Answered

Dear Reader,

Thank you for writing in. Your problem is not at all unusual, unfortunately. Bullying is always seriously wrong but is something that many innocent teenagers like you suffer. I understand how miserable you must be, but <u>don't lose hope</u>. There are ways to end your problem. <u>The bullying will stop</u>.

Bullying is a serious matter and not something you should try to deal with on your own. You don't have to go through this alone. You need others to help you, but they cannot help you unless you tell them. Many victims of bullies keep their misery to themselves. I get the feeling that you haven't told anyone either. I know it might be hard, but tell your parents or a member of your family straight away. They will want to help you and they will understand why you don't want to go to school. Your school probably has an anti-bullying programme, so tell a teacher straight away. Don't be afraid to name the bullies. Everything you tell the teacher will be confidential, so don't be afraid the bullies will make it worse for you if you tell.

While your problem is being sorted out, you might find it helpful to ring a Helpline where you can talk to people who are experienced in helping victims of bullying. They'll understand how you're feeling. You could ring Childline or Victim Support. Remember, bullies are criminals and have to be stopped to save others from suffering as you are. Start acting now! Good Luck.

'We're Here to Help' Ed.

REGISTER

In this task, the students are being asked to write to a frightened thirteen-year-old who needs their help. They need to offer understanding and reassurance, as well as practical advice. Their language should be formal but easily understood, friendly, and comforting.

LAYOUT

To show that you are aware of the purpose of your writing, give your work an appropriate **heading** or **title**. In this case, the students are being asked to write for the problem page of a magazine, so they could write a title such as: '*Your Problems Answered*', or '*Got a Problem? Write to us*'.

Their reply is going to appear in the problem page of the magazine, so it doesn't require the same formal letter layout as in the Persuade task on page 81, where the students were asked to write a letter to an expedition leader.

To make your writing authentic, include an appropriate salutation (opening), such as '*Dear Reader*'. Also sign off appropriately. In a problem page, you wouldn't write '*yours sincerely*' but just a name such as 'Problems Editor', or even just the abbreviation for Editor (Ed.).

PLANNING AND ORGANIZATION

Don't start to write straight away, but think about the task that you've been given. Then make a brief plan of what you will include in the separate paragraphs. Remember that, in the case above, the 'Editor' wants to reassure as well as give advice.

EXAMINER'S COMMENTS

Here are an Examiner's comments on the example student's work. You can use them as a checklist when you write your own response to the task at the end of this unit.

Communication

- ✓ All sentences communicate meaning clearly.
- ✓ There is a clear sense of purpose and audience throughout.
- ✓ There is a personal, reassuring involvement of the Editor, with the use of the personal pronoun '*I*'.
- ✓ The reader is kept involved and is addressed directly and frequently with the second-person pronoun '*you*'.

✓ The register for advice is appropriate with a mix of sympathy, reassurance, and firmness.

✓ Phrases and clauses are chosen to show understanding ('*I know it might be hard*') and reassurance ('*Don't be afraid*').

✓ The vocabulary is appropriate, if unadventurous.

✓ There is the use of imperative verbs to stress the importance of the advice ('<u>*Tell*</u> *your parents*'; '<u>*Start*</u> *acting now!*').

Organization of ideas

✓ The paragraphs are clearly organized.

✓ There are paragraphs of different lengths for different purposes, e.g. short introductory paragraph; longer main paragraph; brief signing-off paragraph.

✓ The advice is coherent, with some development and detail.

Range and accuracy

✓ The heading, salutation (opening), and signing-off are appropriate and accurate.

✓ Some variety of sentence structure is used, e.g. brief emphatic command ('*Start acting now!*'); final verbless sign-off ('*Good Luck*'); simple and complex sentences.

✓ The sentence demarcation is accurate, i.e. full stops and capital letters in the right places.

✓ There are short sentences for effect in the first paragraph, with underlining for further emphasis and reassurance.

✓ Spelling is accurate, including words beginning to show a developed vocabulary, e.g. '*experienced*', '*confidential*', and '*bullies*'.

✓ An exclamation mark is used appropriately.

✓ Clauses are demarcated correctly with commas ('*I know it might be hard, but*').

✓ Apostrophes are correctly used, e.g. '*don't*', '*haven't*'.

YOUR TASK

Now write your response to the following task. You are an advice column writer for the problem page of a magazine and have received the following letter. Write a reply to the letter for the problem page, in which you advise the writer of the letter what to do.

'I am sixteen years old and play in a band. When I've finished my GCSEs, I want to leave school and concentrate on my music, but my parents say I've got to go to college. What should I do?'

WRITING UNIT 4: ANALYSE

INTRODUCTION

Another form of writing which you may be asked to do in the examination involves the analysis of a topic and the presentation of the results of that analysis, often in the form of a report. Look at the example below and the explanation that follows.

> ### STUDENTS' TASK
> A programme researcher is asking young people to help him with his planning for a television series. Write a report for the researcher, in which you analyse the factors that you think affect the quality of family life today.

Here is one student's complete answer:

REPORT FOR PROGRAMME RESEARCHER ON FAMILY LIFE

Family life today is affected by many different factors, ranging from socio-economic and cultural issues to who gets control of the TV remote! Here's my analysis of the factors that I think are important.

Conflict in relationships within the family

The keystone in any family is the relationship between the parents. If parents are happy, the children are more likely to be happy. Arguing or fighting parents put strain on all the relationships in the family. Sour feelings after a row ripple through the household and family life seems to be on a knife-edge for a while. Divorce and family break-up will completely change, and sometimes destroy, family life. The children's view of family life can be permanently affected and they might never see the family as something that brings joy and support.

Parents aren't the only ones who can fight in families. Almost daily fights with my brother raise my mother's stress levels. A 'Kevin the Teenager' brother or an obnoxious daughter with rings in her lip can cause constant battles with parents. All this tension puts enormous strain on the family.

Television and computers

'A family that eats together stays together' goes the saying, but frequently everyone in the family snacks from the microwave in front of the television. Where young people have their own televisions, the family isn't even in the same room and conversation which brings the family together doesn't happen. Being so used to computers can make us expect things to happen at the press of a button, rather than learning how things work. We become impatient with family relationships, too, because we're not prepared to put time into learning to understand each other.

Work

When both parents are in work, it's good for the family income. But employment can come with a price. Long working hours and tired, stressed parents are one reason why family meals often don't happen. Time spent as a family is very valuable, but so is time spent apart (which is why my dad goes in the shed when my mum watches Pop Idol!). There's a crucial balance between personal freedom and space, and the responsibilities and needs of the family. It's hard to get it right.

Jason Cartright aged 15
Oswald Community School, Plymouth

WRITING A REPORT

The assignment above makes a useful comparison with the assignment on page 94. Both assignments ask for a report to be written, but the different contexts influence the tone or register used. The report on page 94 is a straightforward formal report for a head teacher on a year group's **comments** on a proposal for change. In the assignment above, students are being asked to **analyse** those factors which they think affect the quality of family life. This introduces a personal element, so here the writer can:
◆ write in the first person;
◆ use contracted verbs ('*aren't*', '*doesn't*');
◆ include personal experience;
◆ add a touch of humour.

The other conventions of report writing remain, and are:
◆ use of reported speech, not direct speech;
◆ use of some verbs in the passive form, e.g. '*family life <u>can be</u> adversely <u>affected</u> by money problems*'.

ORGANIZATION

Even though the report above is less formal than some you might be asked to write, the organization is still crucial, so that the reader is able to follow it easily. He or she will want to see the main points at a glance.
1. Give your report a sensible, straightforward **title** in either capitals or lower case, e.g. *Report on factors affecting family life*.
2. Plan your report. First of all, jot down a list of what you think are the most important factors, e.g. money worries; illness; step parents; the family house; religion; holidays.

3. Organize your factors under several **headings**, e.g. Relatives; Technology in the home; Employment.
4. Work out how to expand with detail and evidence the effect of the factors you have chosen. In this case, you could include **brief** personal experience, but don't relate anecdotes.
5. Introduce and conclude your report. In this particular instance, the writer is not being asked to conclude with statistical evidence, but a brief introduction and conclusion will shape the report.
6. Write your name at the end and include information which you think might be helpful to the reader. He or she might be interested in your age, whether you're male or female, and probably your school, or your home address.

It is up to you to choose the factors which **you** think are important for that particular report. There are no right or wrong answers: your choice will depend on your personal opinions and experiences. The focus is on your **analysis** of the factors you choose.

EXAMINER'S COMMENTS

Here are an Examiner's comments on the example student's report. You can use them as a checklist when you write your own response to the task at the end of this unit.

Communication

✓ A range of factors is clearly presented.
✓ The purpose of the report is clear and focused throughout.
✓ The introduction is clear and focused, and introduces an appropriate tone of both formality and individuality.
✓ The register combines formality and humour (*'to who gets control of the TV remote!'*) without losing sight of the serious focus.
✓ Humour is well controlled and effective.
✓ An extended vocabulary is used, e.g. *'socio-economic'*; *'obnoxious'*; *'crucial'*.
✓ The analysis of the effects of different factors on family life goes beyond the personal.
✓ Causes and effects are clearly and economically analysed with insight (*'Being so used to computers can make us expect things to happen at the press of a button'*).

✓ There is an appropriate balance between personal experience and the analysis of abstract issues.

✓ There is an effective and punchy concluding sentence.

✓ It is appropriately and helpfully signed off.

✓ There is a varied and well-chosen use of references ('*A 'Kevin the Teenager' brother'; 'A family that eats together stays together'*).

Organization of ideas

✓ The introductory paragraph offers an economical and focused overview as well as a well-judged touch of humour.

✓ The paragraphs are clearly planned and given headings to enhance the effectiveness of the report.

✓ The factors selected are developed, coherent and raise complex issues, e.g. the balance between personal freedom and responsibility within a family.

Range and accuracy

✓ The sentence demarcation is accurate.

✓ There is some variety of sentence structure, used correctly, e.g. brief final sentence; complex sentences with dependent clauses; starting a sentence with a connective for effect ('*But employment can come with a price*').

✓ There is a variety of punctuation, used correctly: exclamation marks; quotation marks; parenthetical brackets; apostrophes; commas to mark off clauses.

✓ There is accurate spelling, including a few ambitious words, e.g. '*crucial*', '*obnoxious*', and many words which show a developed vocabulary, e.g. '*cultural*', '*tension*', '*ripple through*', '*valuable*'.

✓ There is correct use and spelling of the verb 'to affect'.

✓ Verbs are used in the active and passive form.

✓ Apostrophes are used correctly in contracted verbs: '*it's*'; '*there's*'.

> **YOUR TASK**
>
> Now write your own response to the following task. A programme researcher is asking young people to help him with his planning for a television series. Write a report for the researcher in which you analyse the factors which you think affect students' decisions as to whether or not to stay on in education after GCSEs.

WRITING UNIT 5: REVIEW

INTRODUCTION

Review involves looking back and analysing something which has happened in the past, such as a part of your life or a film or play you may have seen. Look at the example below and the explanation that follows.

STUDENTS' TASK

Write an article for your school magazine in which you review your primary school years. Focus on assessing what you feel were your achievements and failures during those years.

Here is one student's complete answer:

My care-free days

Everyone can remember their first day at school. For me it was the most anxious day of my life. I remember the pushing and shoving of children, vast plains of concrete, sky-scraping buildings and never-ending stairs. I didn't know anyone and I was petrified. My first achievement was to find that after a short time, school wasn't really so overwhelming and the buildings weren't as enormous as they seemed on the first day. I was surviving!

I remember my first achievement for work. It was a Smiley Face sticker in my English book and I was so proud showing it to my mum. When we first did multiplication and division, I was completely bewildered and I was scared of our teacher who was thin and very strict. I really battled with those signs and when I finally felt familiar with them, I had a great sense of achievement. I was so pleased with myself and it taught me that I could do something that seemed impossible to start with. I started in the bottom set for maths, but I moved up as I grew more confident and we had a really good teacher called Mrs Hughes.

I loved sport and when I was chosen for the netball team I was over the moon. My mum bought me new kit. We had a very good teacher and he told us about the value of building up your team and not just thinking about yourself. I learned a lot from that and it helped me make really good friends too.

I suppose the only failure of my primary school days was that I never learned to like school dinners. There was a dinner lady who used to try to make me eat horrible things like mince, which I hated. I used to dread dinner times and sometimes I used to wait in the toilets and not go in the dining hall because even the thought of it made me feel sick. I hated that dinner lady and I still hate mince!

Some people say if schooldays are the best of your life, what's the point of living as things are just going to get worse, but I enjoyed my care-free primary school days. Perhaps I'm lucky, but I remember the achievements not the failures.

Kate Divers, Year 10

REGISTER

The above assignment is a review for a school magazine, so, although the language will be formal and not colloquial, the review should be entertaining and lively to read. The personality of the writer should shine through as experiences are reflected upon and assessed as achievements and failures.

WRITING A REVIEW

When you write a **review** of a book you have read, you don't just re-tell the story. You consider it as a whole. You select parts for analysis and interpretation, and you comment on the elements which you think were, for example, particularly gripping or moving. Finally, you offer your overall opinion as to whether the book is worth reading.

Here, the students are asked to **review** not a book but a part of their own lives, focusing on their achievements and failures. In this case, they mustn't just relate events — that would be a narrative account, not a review. They must focus on **issues**, that is achievements and failures, and use **references** to their experiences to illustrate the points they make. In this way, they will get the focus of the question right and write about more than just personal experiences.

ORGANIZATION

1. In tasks like the one above, you should plan your paragraphs carefully. In this case, you could make an 'achievement' column and a 'failure' column. You could then jot down experiences for each and a brief comment on the feelings each gave you. You would then expand this comment with more detail in your full written answer. For example, reading your first book may have given you a feeling of pride and independence, whereas not being chosen for a sports team may have disappointed you.

    Everyone's experiences will be different, so there might be more achievements than failures, or vice versa. As long as there is at least one of each, it doesn't matter because you will have answered the question. What *does* matter is focusing on expanding each comment, *not* on relating the incident.
2. Give your article an interesting title.
3. Introduce your article with a focused, interesting sentence.
4. Conclude with a sentence which expresses your overall view.
5. Put your name and year or class group at the end.

EXAMINER'S COMMENTS

Here are an Examiner's comments on the example student's review. Use them as a checklist when you write a response to the task below.

Communication

✓ A range of achievements and failures is clearly presented.
✓ The purpose of the article is clear and sharply focused on achievements and failures throughout.
✓ The introductory paragraph interests the reader and immediately focuses sharply on the task.
✓ It is effectively concluded and appropriately signed off.
✓ The register is appropriate, with use of the first person.
✓ A range of verbs is used to convey the concept of 'review' ('*I suppose*'; '*I remember*'; '*I learned a lot*').
✓ The review element in the article goes beyond the anecdotal.
✓ The vocabulary is appropriate and some is developed, e.g. '*petrified*'.

Organization

✓ The paragraphs are clearly planned to enhance the effectiveness of the review.
✓ Incidents and memories are appropriately selected to illustrate the issues reviewed.
✓ The introductory paragraph contains interesting detail, as well as a focused review of the first achievement.
✓ A balance is achieved between the explanation of the events and analysis of their significance.

Range and accuracy

✓ The sentence demarcation is accurate.
✓ Simple and complex sentences are accurately constructed.
✓ Brief, emphatic sentences are used for effect ('*I was surviving!*').
✓ There is some variety of punctuation, used correctly: exclamation marks; commas to demarcate clauses or phrases.
✓ The connectives '*and*' and '*but*' are used correctly.
✓ There is accurate spelling of words, which shows the beginnings of a developed vocabulary ('*bewildered*'; '*division*'; '*surviving*').
✓ The key words in the task are spelt correctly ('*achievement*'; '*failure*').

> ### YOUR TASK
>
> Now write your own response to the following task. Write an article for your school magazine in which you review your life so far. Focus on the lessons for life which you feel you have learned over the years.

WRITING UNIT 6: COMMENT

INTRODUCTION

Sometimes you may be asked to comment on something. This could take the form of a formal report. Look at the example below and the explanation that follows.

> ### STUDENTS' TASK
> Your head teacher is proposing to allow students over 16 years old to smoke at break time in an outside area set aside for smokers. Imagine that you are the representative for your year group. Write a report for your head teacher in which you record your year group's comments on the proposal.

Here is one student's complete answer:

COMMENTS FROM YEAR 11 ON THE SMOKING PROPOSAL

Comments in favour of the proposal

A group of pupils, mostly boys, claimed that they would no longer miss lessons to smoke secretly if there were a smoking area. They said that they would not cause trouble if they could smoke at break time and it would also help reduce stress during exam time.

Pupils who had been punished for smoking thought it was a good idea because it would cut down on punishments. Another argument for the proposal was that it would give the smokers a sense of responsibility because they would be treated like adults.

Comments from those who were not in favour of the proposal

It was felt by many that allowing pupils to smoke at school would give the school a bad name. Parents would think that the school was encouraging smoking. The non-smokers said that teachers should protect the health of their pupils, not offer them opportunities to smoke.

It was also felt that lower years would want the age limit reduced to include them. Several pupils thought that having the smoking area might encourage non-smokers to start smoking. They were also afraid that if smoking was allowed in the area, pupils might bring in alcohol and drugs too.

Many pupils thought it would be too difficult to control. Teachers would have to make sure everyone was over 16. The pupils would have to have ID and perhaps their parents' permission too. They thought it would be too much hassle.

Conclusion

Out of 140 pupils in Year 10, 51 were in favour of the proposal and 89 were against it. It is clear that the majority of Year 11 is not in favour of the proposal.

Jonathan Minstrel, Year 11 Representative

WRITING A FORMAL REPORT

In this task, students are asked to record their group's **comments** in a **formal written report**. The year group would need to **review** the proposal first, i.e. discuss its advantages and disadvantages. The representative would take notes, jotting down the points made. Then, after the discussion, he or she would shape the notes into an organized report. The year group's comments would be **colloquial** and probably include plenty of slang. The representative's job would be to avoid their slang and colloquial expressions and express their opinions in **formal language**.

1. Use **reported speech**, not direct speech.
    Direct speech: '"What a stupid idea!" John shouted.'
    Reported speech: 'John felt strongly that it was not a good idea.'
2. Use verbs in their full form, i.e. 'cannot' rather than 'can't'.
3. **Passive voice verbs** are appropriate to formal report writing, so include some in yours.
    Active: 'Some pupils <u>thought</u> the proposal might encourage smokers.'
    Passive: 'It <u>was thought</u> by some that the proposal might encourage smokers.'
4. Write in the third person, i.e. use he/she/it/they

PLANNING AND ORGANIZATION

A report is not a letter, so don't use a letter format. It needs to be clear for the reader to see your main points at a glance, so organization is important.

1. Give your report a clear **title**, e.g. 'Report on Year 11's comments for Mr Fielding'
2. Use **headings** to enable the reader to see your main points easily. The clearest would be, for example, 'Comments in favour of the proposal'; 'Comments against the proposal'.
3. Plan two or three paragraphs underneath each heading. Jot down comments on the proposal and some **reasons** for each comment which you can expand on when you write, e.g. 'Smokers approve: will reduce stress / make them behave better / won't smoke in secret'.
4. **Conclude** your report in a final paragraph headed: 'Conclusion'. In this brief paragraph, sum up the main findings. Use simple statistics rather than vague expressions like 'most' or 'not many', e.g. 'Over 75% were in favour' or '60 out of 83 pupils were against'.
5. Finally, write your name and position (e.g. Year 11 Representative) at the end of the report.

EXAMINER'S COMMENTS

Here are an Examiner's comments on the example student's report. You can use them as a checklist when you write your own response to the task at the end of this unit.

Communication

✓ The meaning of every sentence is clear.
✓ The purpose and audience of the report is clear throughout.
✓ The formal register is appropriate for a report.
✓ The use of reported speech is appropriate and both active and passive verbs are used.
✓ The conclusion is clear and to the point.
✓ The vocabulary is appropriate, if unadventurous – '*hassle*' could be replaced with more developed vocabulary such as 'difficult and time-consuming'; '*a bad name*' with 'a poor reputation'.

Organization of ideas

✓ The title is clear.
✓ The report is clearly signed off.
✓ The paragraphs are given clear and focused headings.
✓ The student's comments are coherent, arranged sensibly and reasonably well supported with some explanation and detail.
✓ The paragraphs are brief, as appropriate to a report.

Range and accuracy

✓ The report layout is accurate.
✓ There is variation in the choice of verbs introducing reported comments, e.g. '*claimed that*', '*said that*', '*were afraid that*'.
✓ The formal sentences are accurately constructed.
✓ Simple connectives are used correctly in complex sentences to link clauses, e.g. '*because*', '*and*'.
✓ The demarcating commas in the phrase '*mostly boys*' are correct.
✓ The apostrophe in the plural possessive noun is correctly used in '*parents' permission*'.
✓ The spelling is accurate, including words beginning to show a developed vocabulary, e.g. '*responsibility*', '*opportunities*', '*alcohol*'.

YOUR TASK

Now write your own response to the following task. Your head teacher is proposing a change in the school shop. He or she wants to allow only fruit, sandwiches and fruit drinks to be sold there. As your year group representative, write a report for him or her in which you record your year group's comments on the proposal.